CLEVELAND RADIO
Tales

CLEVELAND RADIO *Tales*

Stories from the Local Radio Scene
of the 1960s, '70s, '80s, and '90s

Mike & Janice Olszewski

GRAY & COMPANY, PUBLISHERS
CLEVELAND

Gray & Company, Publishers
www.grayco.com

ISBN: 978-1-938441-90-5
Printed in the U.S.A.
1

This book is dedicated to
Vinnie Anderson, with many thanks for
years of inspiration, loyalty and friendship.

Contents

Preface 9

"This station should kiss my ass . . ." 13

"Shooting pool with a rope!" 33

"You're never going to make it in this business!" 41

"You stay in that world and you'll be a bum . . ." 52

"Get down, dammit!" 66

WKRP in . . . Willoughby 70

"I didn't saddle up to come in second!" 74

Fired for Being Herself 85

Meeting the Beatles 96

The Buzzard—Behind the Curtain 100

Belly Up To The Bar 105

The Backstage Pass 111

"There's evil in this building" 125

"Good line, smart ass" 132

Theater of the Mind 136

Power to the People! 145

Air Pirates 151

Mama, Don't Let Your Cowboys Grow Up to Be Deejays . . 158

At Your Service 162

Short Circuits 169

"You're scaring my kids!" 175

"Bouncy, Bouncy!" 179

The Birth of the Buzzard 185

Acknowledgments 189

Preface

WHEN I WAS A kid, my grandmother would tell me about "this thing called vaudeville." In the days before radio and television, when movies were really just starting to come into their own, vaudeville theaters were everywhere. Playhouse Square had the most elaborate houses, but Keith's 105th drew big crowds near University Circle, and even small towns like Kent and Chagrin Falls had shows every week. Bob Hope, the Marx Brothers, W.C. Fields, Houdini—they were all part of huge traveling shows with ten, fifteen, even twenty acts on the bill.

But times change, and as more options arose vaudeville just faded away. Sort of. When TV reared its head, Ed Sullivan basically put on a vaudeville show every Sunday night until that ran its course as well. Even so, my grandmother had wonderful memories of those days and loved to share them.

That's how we learn about each other and the times we lived in. We pass on stories like folklore and it's the poignant, or funny, or sad, or the stuff with an ironic twist, that stays with us.

A few years back, I put out a book titled *Radio Daze: Stories from the Front in Cleveland's FM Air Wars*. It was important to me to document that whole era in an impartial way because it was a vital part of Northeast Ohio history. The book got a lot of attention, including a mention from Howard Stern. But the greatest compliment I got came from a programmer who said, "I didn't like what I read, but it was accurate."

Every time I did a talk at a library or a book signing, folks would come up and ask about their favorite stories. They wanted more, and not just from the FM side. Every generation had its favorite stations and personalities, whether it came out of a transistor radio or a quad system.

You wanted more? Well, you're holding them in your hand.

When you worked in radio, you often found yourself in unusual situations, and sometimes they didn't turn out quite the way you expected. I've got a couple of my own stories like that to share.

Back in early 1988, I was in New York covering the third annual Rock and Roll Hall of Fame inductions at the Waldorf Astoria for WMMS. It was going to be a long night, and I was scheduled to file reports early the next day from the studios of NBC's Source Radio Network. About two in the afternoon I got a call from the station with a request from one of the local record guys.

That was a big night. Mick Jagger was inducting the Beatles, Bruce Springsteen was introducing Bob Dylan, Elton John was there for the Beach Boys. And no one was paying attention to the Drifters, who were also being inducted into the hall. They had a box set coming out that covered their whole career, and the promo guy asked if I could do a quick interview. In return, he would be glad to do the station a favor and that usually meant a hot new release before any other station. You couldn't say no, and I was glad to help anyway.

I put on my tux, grabbed the recorder, and got to the Waldorf just as the Drifters were finishing their rehearsal.

"Hey guys! Got time for a quick interview?"

Johnny Moore said he had a few minutes, and we sat down by the side of the stage. I asked Moore if he remembered playing Cleveland much. He let out a little laugh and said, "Are you kidding? I went to John Adams High School. They saw me singing at the Dove Lounge when I was a kid."

John Adams? The Dove Lounge? On Liberty Boulevard? I told him I grew up right around the corner on Harvard near East 131st.

Moore opened his eyes really wide and said, "You mean by Odziemski's Hardware?" I could see that store from my house!

For the next hour we talked about the Avalon Theater, drinking milk shakes at Rhoton's, the train tracks along Miles Road, and so many other places in our old neighborhood. We even determined that we were in the same place at the same time, when the Woolworth's burned down on a frigid Saturday morning.

Eventually, we both had to leave.

"This was so cool!" Moore said. "Somebody from my neighborhood is here to see me go in the hall. I can't thank you enough!" Big hug and we said goodbye.

Later that night, there was Johnny Moore singing onstage backed by George Harrison, Ringo Starr, Mary Wilson of the Supremes, and some of the biggest names in the industry. But six hours before he was talking about a hardware store in Cleveland, and was loving every minute of it. Got to admit that I did, too!

Another interview has stayed with me, for a far different reason. A few years later, I had a similar call from a book publicist, again, in need of a favor. WMMS had a long-running public affairs show called *Jabberwocky* (Murray Saul had been one of the original hosts). It also ran on WHK as *Cleveland Upfront*. You'd hear local politicians, people from all walks of life, and the occasional author. If it was interesting, it got on the air. That's why the publicist called.

She had a book titled *Who Killed Martin Luther King?: The True Story by the Alleged Assassin*, supposedly written by James Earl Ray. That's right, James Earl Ray, the assassin, and he was doing phone interviews from prison. No one wanted to talk to him, and I told her she could put me in that group, too.

She said, "Look, no one thinks this book is going to sell, but I still have to do the publicity." She said she didn't even care if we aired it. Okay, I said, let's do it—"but you owe me!"

They get him on the phone, I'm rolling tape in the production studio and it's the same old story. He said he wasn't a racist, some clown named Raoul hired him to smuggle contraband and he ended up in Memphis. He wanted the case re-opened and for the U.S. to chase down Raoul and find the real killers.

A few minutes into the interview it struck me that maybe the case should have been re-opened. Don't get me wrong—I'm sure Ray killed MLK. His fingerprints were on the rifle. He even confessed (though he later recanted). But consider this: Ray was able to pull off the crime of the century just a few hundred feet from the Lorraine Motel, escape an international manhunt and make it not only to Canada but to England where they caught him a few months later. You'd have to be pretty smart to pull that off. Again, smart doesn't mean good, and judging by the way he answered my questions I can say that James Earl Ray was neither. He was dumb as a rock, and maybe he did have some help. I think the only work he ever did on a book was with crayons. I hung up the phone and thought about that odd interview for days.

Lots of folks in radio have similar stories. This book is aimed at preserving that history from the folks who made Cleveland radio happen. This is a book about radio people and the reasons they were so special to us listeners. It's stuff that happened behind the scenes, when the mics were off—even at tiny stations with a handful of listeners.

Some of the names in these stories you'll remember, others you won't, and some you probably never heard. But think of them as part of a larger picture, an audio mosaic that entertained us and informed us.

And maybe years from now, we'll be saying, "We used to have this thing called radio . . ."

One more thing: There are plenty of stories in this book about excessive behavior. This is only an accurate reflection of what happened at the time and is not an endorsement.

—Mike Olszewski

"This station should kiss my ass..."

The Bizarre World of Count John Manolesco

WHEN AM RADIO WAS still king, WERE was a powerhouse. It went on the air in 1948 and had a staff as good as any in the country. Disc jockeys like Tommy Edwards, Phil McLean, Carl Reese, and especially Bill Randle helped define popular music and gave major boosts to the careers of the Everly Brothers, Elvis Presley, and even the Mormon Tabernacle Choir. Bob West, Walt Heinrich, and others rounded out a top-notch group that gave the competition a lot to deal with on a daily basis. But it still had its challenges.

The 1300 signal was terrible. It was 5000 watts and directional, meaning the signal was aimed at a certain part of the listening audience. By the time it was fed up the antenna, it was probably 3500 watts and couldn't be heard much outside Cuyahoga County. At that time Cleveland was the eighth biggest city in the U.S., but by the late 1960s FM stereo was starting to get noticed and color TVs were flying off the shelf. The writing was on the wall for music on AM radio.

Bill Randle remained popular, but his audience was aging. He was doing his "Swap and Shop" show where listeners would call in to sell and trade things. Ratings dropped and that usually means a format change. In 1972, management brought in a guy from California who called himself "the Fresno Flash!" His name was Gary Dee, and controversial talk was his specialty. "People Power" was born. That didn't sit well with Randle, who still had pull at the station. Management installed an expensive shower for him in the second-floor rest room, but Randle wanted no part of Gary Dee's style of radio and quit the station two days after the shower was installed.

Dee hit the ground running. He took on Cleveland City Council, racial tension—any topic that would get him noticed. He sparred with Council President George Forbes, who would later get his own show on WERE and who likely saw past Dee's facade. Gary Dee was bright. He had a master's degree and even taught school for a time before getting into radio, but his shtick was a low-rent hillbilly from Hope, Arkansas who said things that most people were afraid to say out loud. He would use inflammatory, racially charged language, but no one who knew him thought he was a racist. The joke was the number of people who would call to agree with him and add to the conversation. His show was based on mocking the stupidity of a large segment of the audience.

When time came for a well-deserved vacation for Dee, station management needed someone to fill in who would keep hi s audience intact. They heard about a guy out of Canada, an astrologer who also claimed to be a vampire: Count John Manolesco.

The timing was right. In 1973, the film *The Exorcist* was a box-office smash, and WERE was ready to exploit the growing interest in the supernatural. Manolesco had an accent like Bela Lugosi and a very colorful background. Yeah, he really was born near the castle of the real Count Dracula, Vlad the Impaler. He held degrees from McGill University in Canada and the London School of Economics, but the station couldn't verify his claim that Winston Churchill had arranged a scholarship in exchange for his services predicting Nazi war plans during World War II.

John Webster was programming WERE at the time, and he remembers that story very well. Webster recalls Manolesco claiming in that thick Romanian accent, "Hitler had his own astrologer. I told da prime minister what da Nazi"—he pronounced it *Nozzi*—"planet watcher vas telling his boss."

Later, Webster said: "Fifty years after the war ended, the British government confirmed that Churchill really did use three astrologers who reported about Hitler's state of mind and war plans! There were no details provided on the astrologers' accuracy." Or their identities.

Count John Manolesco played up his Transylvanian
roots, but his true appeal was his twisted view of reality.

WERE offered Manolesco a very generous contract, but that
wasn't enough. Manolesco insisted that the station managers had
to meet him at the Beverly Hilton Hotel in Los Angeles for a contract signing to take place at precisely 11:27 a.m., Pacific Standard
Time, February 27, 1974. Webster recalls Manolesco saying, "I have
calculated da planetary alignments for dat moment and find it's
perfect for beginning a most prosperous relationship."

The WERE bosses complained that the gas shortage, which was
at its peak at the time, would make travel from the Los Angeles

Airport very difficult. But Manolesco, after making certain calculations, advised his future employers to take a certain flight and "Everything vill be fine. Trust my advice!"

When the station general manager and program director arrived in L.A., they found an agency which rented vehicles with a full tank of gas, more than enough fuel to get them to the hotel and back. The trip took them past long lines of hundreds of cars and trucks waiting to buy a few gallons of precious gasoline. The contract was signed on time and the station managers returned to Cleveland much less skeptical of Manolesco's predictive ability.

Manolesco had an interesting look: A shock of long white hair and a long, thick beard, and he wore his belt well below the elastic band of his boxer shorts. Occasionally, the count would wear one of his black capes. He had a long cape for formal wear and a shorter one for more casual occasions. Sadly, the other hosts were not impressed.

Manolesco was a poseur, a charlatan, an actor, and one of the greatest showmen to ever crack a microphone. Some didn't see it that way, including the Cleveland Catholic Diocese.

"Within a month," Webster says, "the Catholic newspaper the *Universe Bulletin* warned in a front-page story of 'Poisonous Hokum on WERE,' suggesting that participating in the Manolesco program was a mortal sin. Later that year, that same paper announced that WERE would no longer be allowed to broadcast the Christmas eve midnight mass from the Cathedral of St. John. The station had long wanted to cancel the broadcast, but didn't because the station didn't want to offend the church."

The diocese certainly wasn't going to like what the count had planned next: an in-studio exorcism!

Webster says that Manolesco primed his audience, saying, "God is on our side! Ve shall now dedicate ourselves to fighting da Devil" and asked for candidates during his daily show. He personally interviewed them in the station's conference room, which he decorated in black velvet with a crucifix on every wall.

"The Count was smoking cigarettes through a foot-long holder,"

Webster recalls, "was dressed in the black robes and collar of a priest, and sprinkled each applicant with holy water that was stolen from Catholic churches all over town. Plus, he was waving a crucifix—and that was just a rehearsal!"

The interviews went on for about a week, and Manolesco selected thirteen candidates and several alternates.

"On the day of the broadcast, everyone assembled in the conference room, where chairs were arranged in a circle," Webster says. "An announcer/director was hidden in a curtained corner with a full view of the room. When the network news ended, the announcer stated, 'The following program is presented for its entertainment value only. The views and opinions expressed on this program are not necessarily those of WERE, its management, and sponsors.' And he added, 'I give you my word that I shall truthfully report what I see.'"

The conference room door opened and Manolesco strode in, carrying a large incense burner. His white hair and beard had been brushed away from his face to form a halo that contrasted with his black robes to create an eerie iridescence. His crucifix, now on a golden chain, dangled around his neck. As a low, hypnotic drumbeat was piped into the room, he began reading from the *Catholic Rite of Exorcism* pamphlet, published in Rome and provided to priests all over the world.

The announcer, now speaking in a low, suspenseful voice, faithfully described what he saw and noted, 'The candidates seem mesmerized. Some seem agitated and have begun to perspire."

Manolesco continued to walk around the room, looking sternly into the eyes of each candidate, sprinkling more holy water and murmuring the Lord's Prayer. The announcer blurted out, "Dr. Manolesco has suddenly spun around and is approaching a woman in the circle. He is holding his crucifix like a shield. Let's listen."

In his thick Romanian accent, Manolesco shouted, "Satan is here! He hides like a coward. I command you, in da name of Jesus Christ, the son of God, leave dis woman, leave dis room, return forever to hell!"

"Manolesco is sprinkling the woman with holy water as he prays over her," the announcer explained, "and, my god, she has begun to shake and is trying to shove her chair backwards, away from him. Her eyes are filled with what can only be described as hatred."

The announcer fell silent as the woman started shrieking "Get away from me!" in a deep and frightening voice. She lunged at Manolesco as he pressed the crucifix to her forehead. The woman fell back as if she'd been burned and then slumped in her chair, whimpering. That was a good sign to Manolesco. "Da demon has left. You are free." Manolesco was now speaking softly, and comforted the woman while checking her pulse and nodding to the announcer. Then: "This rite of exorcism will continue on WERE after these messages."

The program continued for three hours with a few breaks for news and commercials. More than half the participants seemed genuinely affected by the ceremony. Two vomited when Manolesco touched them with holy water and the crucifix. Three had no apparent effects, and they prayed along with the Count. But not all the weird stuff was happening just in that makeshift studio.

"The most amazing thing that happened that day took place in WERE's master control room," says Webster. "Two tape recorders were set up to record the proceedings, one Ampex professional machine and one Sony archive machine. The Ampex burned out a transformer and stopped recording moments after the first woman was sprinkled with holy water. The Sony machine's long play tape jammed at the same time! The engineering staff looked over the machines and said there was no reason for the malfunctions."

Manolesco had his own theory. "Da work of Satan. No doubt about it!"

WERE's ratings soared. Along with Dee and Manolesco, the station's lineup included Merle Pollis, Howie Lund, and a large cast of over-the-top talk show hosts. Every host tried to outdo the others. Lund even did a show in the nude (much to the surprise of his guests that day!).

But the sales staff struggled to turn the ratings into revenue. It was too controversial. Management often couldn't meet payroll and would occasionally offer the staff products it got in trade from sponsors. There were some great deals, like a Sony Trinitron television, the best TV set on the market, for $100. Gary Dee's producer, Bob Gott, recalls seeing a notice posted for "A house trailer and a side of beef. Best offer." But you can't keep a station on the air with no money. WERE ended People Power and changed formats to all-news in 1975. Gary Dee went to WHK with its exceptional sales staff and generated a mountain of money for owner Malrite Communications.

But what about Manolesco?

The Count wasn't stupid. He got an attorney and negotiated a separation agreement that stated if WERE ever went back to a talk format, he would be called back. Five years later, when word got around that the all-news experiment had failed and the station was returning to talk, Manolesco showed up, waving that piece of paper.

WERE put Manolesco on from 9 to midnight, and he picked up right where he left off. When the Arbitron ratings were released, no one believed what they saw. The morning and afternoon news blocks held their audience, but the talk segments went through the roof! Some day parts quadrupled their ratings. That evening, Manolesco walked into the middle of the newsroom, held his hand above his head, and yelled at the top of his lungs with his heavy Romanian accent, "This station should kiss my ass for making it go talk!" Most people agreed.

The Count had returned to Cleveland from Studio City, California, leaving behind his wife, whom he referred to as "Pussycat." Not long after his return, he asked reporter Andy Oeftering if he would like "an expenses-paid vacation for you and a companion to Calee-fornia?" Just bring back a few cases of expensive wine and some other things from the Count's apartment, he was told. Oeftering was just out of college and it seemed like a good deal. Manolesco gave him and a young lady plane tickets and credit cards and detailed instructions: Pick up the items when Pussycat

Manolesco's thick Romanian accent and outrageous behavior not only made him a ratings sensation, they probably saved WERE from certain doom.

wasn't home, load them into Manolesco's RV, which was parked in the garage, and drive back.

The two landed in California and got a ride to Manolesco's apartment in heavy rain. Pussycat was nowhere in sight, so they loaded the RV and left, following Manolesco's detailed map through the deep south. The rain followed them the entire trip. Only later, after the RV broke down and Oeftering got hurt trying to fix it, did he learn that Manolesco sent them through the south so that they could gas up at stations where his charge cards were still good.

And possibly to avoid the police. It turned out that Manolesco was retrieving stuff that would have been community property in his upcoming divorce.

Oeftering checked himself into a hospital, but the Count refused to pay him additional expenses because he had drunk one of his bottles of wine. Manolesco went on and on to anyone who would listen that Oeftering was a "communist," a "socialist" and would feel his wrath. Oeftering just bugged him until he squared up with him. It wasn't the last time the two would lock horns.

Oeftering was hosting some friends at his home in Lakewood, and they were listening to Manolesco, who had organized a panel to discuss the history of marijuana use and the "opium eaters" of the early 1800s. As usual, the Count was making up some of the history as he went along, and Oeftering had had enough. In those days, radio reporters had a device called a Voice Track that they could screw onto the mouthpiece of a telephone to make their voices clearer for live reports. Oeftering excused himself, left the room and a minute later his friends heard him on air, clear as a bell, stating, "Count, your show is ridiculous, your panel is a joke, your history is rife with mistakes and I believe you should apologize to your audience and resign your commission!"

Manolesco was taken back by the clarity of the line but he recognized the voice, and the two started arguing along with the panel. The party guests just sat there taking in the surreal moment, clouded by alcohol. Finally, after being talked into a corner he couldn't get out of, Manolesco claimed the "caller must be on the Mary-wanna" and hung up. Seconds later Oeftering walked back in, took his seat and resumed his conversation. It was as if he had raced downtown and back in mere seconds.

Manolesco always seemed to be promoting some twisted product or idea. He claimed he could cast his shadow and make it stick on the wall. He frequently played host to Stanton Friedman, the UFO expert, and delved into conspiracies long before Art Bell on network radio. For one of his side businesses, Manolesco became the exclusive distributor for a Romanian mineral water.

It tasted so vile it was undrinkable, and he had cases of it stacked to the ceiling at his apartment at the Park. During one show while Manolesco was hawking the water, he was told that a caller was on the line who was very happy with the product. "Quickly! Put him on!" The caller, who sounded very stoned, said he put it in his bong when he smoked weed and it cleaned the pipe as he used it. Maybe Manolesco wasn't listening carefully but loudly proclaimed, "You see! It's also an effective cleaning agent!"

Then there was the water-powered car. When gas prices soared in the early 1980s, Manolesco claimed to have found an engineer who had invented a device that separated hydrogen from water. Manolesco actually had one installed in his car; his dashboard was fitted with a series of toggle switches that had to be triggered in sequence or the hydrogen would build up and explode. He was looking for investors—until his car was stolen. Manolesco frantically called the station to say the thief was riding in a time bomb and should pull over immediately. Not long after, Cleveland Police called to say the car had been found on an east side street. The thief apparently heard the warning, dumped the car, and ran. Any potential investors dried up after the threat of lawsuits from hydrogen explosions.

The Count's ratings continued to climb, and he came to the attention of the Mutual Broadcasting Network. Larry King was their star attraction (before he went to CNN), and he ruled the airwaves overnight. Mutual was looking to offer syndicated shows in other day parts, and word got back to WERE that they'd give Manolesco a shot if he got a 20-share in the ratings. Well, Manolesco did it! He scored huge numbers with older demographics, but Larry King wasn't exactly courting teenagers. Mutual agreed to give the Count a tryout filling in for King when he went on vacation.

It was a disaster.

Networks run a tight ship. Everything is done in a certain way at a certain time with an eye on the clock at all times. That wasn't Manolesco's kind of radio. At WERE, he would let a conversation go 40 minutes and then play 15 minutes of commercials. That wasn't the way management wanted it done, but with his ratings they weren't about to argue. Every few minutes Manolesco would interrupt the commercial flow and say in his thick accent, "Okay, now dis!" or, "Here's some more. Just stay there."

Mutual Broadcasting did things differently, and it was a long week for both sides. The guest for the final night was singer Freda Payne. The Count didn't know her and didn't care.

"So, girlie. Who are you?" he asked. "Why are you on Manolesco's show?"

"I'm Freda Payne. I'm a singer." This was not a happy guest.

"And what do you sing?"

"Well," she shot back, "are you familiar with 'Band of Gold'?"

"Is that your band? What kind of music do you play?"

The interview quickly degenerated, and Manolesco announced, "Right! Freda, we're going to do astrology." This was his habit at WERE when topics bored him. For the next hour, the Count read astrology charts, occasionally asking, "What do you think about that, Freda?"

That ended Manolesco's network radio career, but his career in Cleveland was about to take a bizarre turn.

*   *   *

A personal note from Mike: I worked at WERE at that time, and saw it first-hand. Despite the older demographics of talk radio, most of the people in the newsroom were young, and they listened to FM rock. This was around the time when Akron's Devo had made a huge splash with their hit "Whip It," a simple tune with a catchy hook and some very weird lyrics.

I noticed that there really wasn't much instrumentation to the song, and there were breaks with no vocals, and this gave me an idea. Chances were the music could be patched together without the vocals. I had a plan.

Production guys are a special bunch. They have trained ears and can get very creative with a razor blade and grease pencil. That's the way we used to edit tape. I tried to splice together a backing track, but that took patience and a certain talent I didn't have. But WERE had a couple of guys who did, Scott Cunningham and Jim Mehrling.

Cunningham did production at night and recorded Manolesco's promos for his upcoming shows. The Count wanted to get out of the station as soon as he could after his shift, so he just raced through everything he was asked to read. He didn't ask, he just read the copy and left. Scott and I talked about my idea on a Friday afternoon, and when I came in for my Saturday morning shift Cunningham had the first version of Manolesco's version of "Whip It"—pronounced "Vhip it."

We didn't want Manolesco to know we had tricked him, so we only played the song for friends. Then Ray Hoffman heard it.

WERE had no shortage of characters. Ray Hoffman was a straight-laced newsman during the week, but his Sunday talk show was surreal, with a cast that might make David Lynch envious.

There was Hoffman's imaginary evil twin brother, Rex, a big band leader who traveled from city to city causing trouble. Cosmo the Tailor would stop in with tales of the clothing he created for has-been stars, always heavy with sequins. He had a rivalry with another count named Chernikov who was deposed in the Bolshevik Revolution and was played by a visually impaired listener known only as "Sam the Blind Man." "The Sneak" would drop by, in various stages of sobriety, to discuss baseball, football, roller derby, and professional wrestling and how he bet with his bookie on all of them. He would occasionally update everyone on a ladies' "shirts and skins" bowling machine league he followed. A woman claiming to be actress Rula Lenska's sister, Ruta, would call in to describe her glamorous life until her husband called from the trailer park to say, "Woman, get home!"

When country singer Slim Whitman's career was revived in the early 1980s, Hoffman aired some mock recordings allegedly made by Whitman. (These eventually caught the attention of the singer's management—and they loved them!) There was "Wind Over Gaza" by Slim and the West Bank Rhythm Boys, supposedly sang and yodeled in some weird Middle Eastern tongue (which was actually a tape of Whitman singing backwards). The follow-up song was "By the Waters of the Minnetonka," a recording of Whitman crooning while large objects were flung into the babbling waters of a nearby waterfall. Hoffman was even asked to host Whitman's Richfield Coliseum show, and the singer was delighted with the huge response.

We thought no one listened to the radio on football Sundays, including the management, so it didn't matter what we put on. (Years later I had a guy come up to say he would drive around the city all afternoon alone listening to the show so he could hear it without his kids bothering him.)

Hoffman, I knew, would enjoy the Count's cover of "Whip It," so I played it for him in the newsroom. He insisted we put it on the air.

The phones exploded!

The way Manolesco stressed certain lines, like "Break you mama's back," outraged some people and drew wild applause from others. We thought that would be the end of it, though.

Wow! Were we wrong!

The next day, management started getting calls. Some complained about the filthy lyrics; others wanted to know where to buy it. Management didn't listen to Hoffman's show, so they just figured it was one of Manolesco's bits. That Monday night someone called the Count's show to ask about the song, and he didn't know what they were talking about. He did some detective work, and I got a call the next day.

"SOME FRIEND YOU ARE!"

I knew the voice and accent but had never heard it at that volume. This could get real ugly real quick, I thought.

"I understand you put my voice on a contemporary tune."

"It was just a joke," I stammered.

"Why didn't you give it to me for my show?! Put it in my mail slot."

That night, Manolesco's guests were former Cleveland Mayor Ralph Perk and Congresswoman Mary Rose Oakar. Five minutes into the show, the Count said, "Did you know I am a rock and roll star?" He played the song, and the floodgates opened. It wasn't a lot of calls—it was a tsunami of listeners and every one of them had an opinion. Any topic Perk and Oakar had been planning to address went out the window. The only thing they and the callers wanted to talk about was "Whip it."

It happened again the next night and the night after that, and took on a life of its own. Bob Gott aired it on WGCL. The college stations asked for dubs. It was obvious that Count Manolesco had found a new audience.

The count demanded a follow-up, so along with Jim Mehrling we put together a version of Rick Derringer's "Rock and Roll Hoochie Koo." Manolesco announced that we were now his band, "Count Manolesco and the No-Counts," and he was ready to tour. We even had some informal promotional shots done, and the *Cleveland Press* issued a fold-out poster with women hanging all over Manolesco.

Paul McCartney's brother, Mike, stopped by WERE, heard "Whip It," and asked for a copy to take back to Liverpool. National recording artist Donnie Iris did a special intro for "Rock and Roll Hoochie Koo."

Meanwhile, the Count added to his own legend by hawking a serum called Gerovital that he claimed was a pharmaceutical fountain of youth that he had injected into his bare buttocks twice a day. But the second injection was scheduled in the 11 o'clock hour of his show and he would ask whoever was in the studio to give him the injection! Many a guest got a surprise at 11 p.m. when he handed them a syringe and bent over the console.

Jim Mehrling is a production genius. That word is overused, but anyone who has worked with Jim agrees it applies. His sense of creativity is unmatched. When Manolesco demanded yet another song, Jim decided to do an original. It's unlikely Jim had ever heard a punk rock song, but he put together a musical bed patch-ing together bits from a Ramones album. He wrote some lyrics, Manolesco recorded them, and the result was "Gerovital."

Manolesco desperately wanted to perform his songs on stage and even had Buddy Maver from the Agora and Jane Scott from the *Plain Dealer* on his show to discuss his options. Plus, he was no stranger to record shops, having put out a series of astrology albums years before (copies show up on eBay to this day). He insisted that WERE management put out an album to capitalize on his new fame. When they explained how much it would cost in production and licensing fees, the Count shrugged it off and demanded they get the project underway. Then management said, "Fine. And you'll pay the cost of any albums that don't sell." Manolesco paused for a second, and said "It was just an idea!"

He was still a rock star in his own studio.

*   *   *

Manolesco continued to draw a huge audience doing what he did best, playing the outrageous Transylvanian aristocrat turned crazed talk show host. It's when he took the act on the road that anything could happen.

Manolesco lived just three blocks down the street from WERE, at the Park Apartments at East 12th and Chester Avenue. The station was at East 15th. He could walk to work yet always drove so he wouldn't have to deal with the people who hung around outside the bar across the street next to the Greyhound station.

Every now and then he would have to do a remote broadcast, and make no mistake, Manolesco hated remotes!

Geauga Lake Amusement Park was about 45 minutes outside the city in Portage County. The owner decided to try to extend the season by holding an Old World Oktoberfest—in the middle of October! They bought a lot of time on WERE and demanded Manolesco do a live remote that Friday as part of the buy.

October is always chilly, but no one expected it to be this cold. A large tent was set up with rows of chairs, and a propane heater was brought in to keep it as warm as possible. Here's the problem:

This was a big tent, Manolesco would be broadcasting live until midnight, and the heater had to be set at half power so the propane would last the evening—barely.

Sally Lewis was the engineer, and she hated working remotes with the Count. He was crabby, uncooperative, demanding, and always found something to gripe about. She wasn't about to let him get to her. Sally set up the Count's microphone and made it as simple as possible to avoid any headaches. Not likely. Predictably, Manolesco was in a foul mood when he arrived early at 6 p.m. "It's too cold! Turn up the heat!" Folks tried to warn him, but Manolesco started causing a scene. At that point they gave him anything he wanted.

Then it was Sally's turn. Speaking very slowly and deliberately she said, "Listen carefully. All you have to do is to flip this switch when you turn on your mike. The light will be green. When it's off the light will be red. You'll go with green and stop with red. Just like a car. Don't switch to red if you want the mike on. Switch to green. Green on, red off. Got it?"

Manolesco glared at her and barked, "Right! And where do I make a pee? In the booshes?!"

Everyone left, and Manolesco was on his own. All he had to do was flip a switch back and forth until midnight. It was cold, and the rain started to come down heavy, and the long night had begun.

By 8 p.m. the rain was so heavy that vendors were packing up, and management shut down the park for the night. The only people stopping by were park employees seeking shelter from the rain. Manolesco interviewed most of them just to fill time, and even played "Whip it" a few times to eat up the clock.

By 9 o'clock the park was empty except for Manolesco and security people, and that's when the propane heater coughed a few times and stopped. There was no one to take over back at the station, and Manolesco spent the rest of the show cold and alone in the tent, cursing Geauga Lake and WERE management and describing the horrible conditions. Listeners could hear the howling winds and pounding rain. It was like an audio version of

Count Manolesco and the No-Counts! Despite the fact that the band only worked out of a production studio, Manolesco was convinced it could be a top concert draw. *Joe Jasztremski*

The Blair Witch Project, and some of the funniest radio ever heard on that station.

Not long after, all the WERE talk show hosts were sent to a day-long charity remote at Randall Park Mall, which at the time was the biggest shopping mall in North America. There would be a lot of people, it was a half an hour from downtown, and it was indoors. But Manolesco still hated remotes, and was no more cooperative than he had been at Geauga Lake. With "Whip It" booming through the mall at the beginning of every hour, Manolesco made the best of what he saw as a bad situation and read horoscopes live on the air for charity. An elderly woman stopped by and, after handing over a check for $25, was told she was going on a long and terrible journey. "That will be just the beginning of a torturous ordeal. I hate to take your money. Next!" About an hour later a visibly distraught woman approached the table and Manolesco put her on the air. Sobbing, she explained that the woman Manolesco had said would go on a horrendous journey had collapsed and was pronounced dead at the hospital. She warned him the check could not be cashed. Manolesco proudly crowed on the air, "You see! And they laugh at astrology!"

Sadly, Manolesco never got his wish to be a geriatric rock star. He was diagnosed with cancer, and died in January 1983. The on-air tributes at WERE included his musical projects, and his pallbearers were three astrologers and three reporters. He was buried in a small plot near a trailer park on Cleveland's west side. The staff joked that his gravestone should say, "Now dis!"

The Count's replacement at WERE was Morton Downey, Jr., who would go on to a long and highly publicized career after he left Cleveland, but he never caught on in Manolesco's old spot. In fact, Downey would never even mention his stay in Cleveland in any of his biographical material. He just couldn't capture the Count's magic.

*   *   *

A personal note from Mike: The story continues after Manolesco's death. In 2005, I got a call at home from a guy named Orin Gubkin. Orin was a young college broadcaster who probably wasn't even alive when Manolesco was around. Orin asked if I was involved with Manolesco's "Whip It." The copy at Cleveland State's station and been played so much it was unlistenable, and there were still a few old air checks with people talking about the song. He was fascinated with Manolesco's delivery and wanted to offer a proposal.

Devo fans gather every year for a convention called the "Devotional." There's music and lectures and sometimes members of the band attend. Orin was in touch with the promoters and suggested we reform Count Manolesco and the No-Counts to perform "Whip It" at the convention. I explained that could be difficult. The No-Counts weren't really a band, and the lead singer was dead. But the wheels started turning.

I called Jim Mehrling and Scott Cunningham and we met at a restaurant in Parma. It was like that scene in Stephen King's *It*, when the grown-up kids meet again to deal with Pennywise, the evil clown. Never in a million years would we have guessed we'd still be talking about that song so many years later. The private joke had taken on a life of its own.

I was surprised that the promoters were even interested. Years before, when Manolesco was inducted into a broadcasters' hall of fame, I sent off a copy of "Whip it" to Devo's Mark Mothersbaugh for a taped testimonial, but I never heard anything back. Still, here we were eating hamburgers and drinking beer and trying to figure out how we could make this happen. I contacted a drummer I knew, Eric Leas, and he rounded up a guitar player and a bassist. Cunningham also played guitar and I brought an electric keyboard to fill out the sound. Mehrling isolated Manolesco's voice from old tapes and we set up a couple of rehearsals. We were heading to the Devotional.

The convention was held at a bar in Akron, the Lime Spider, and featured a day-long tribute to Devo with music, vendors and a whole series of stage presentations. The place was packed and when our time came we took the stage. We looked like a traditional band, with one major exception: Jim Mehrling came out dressed like a mad scientist, complete with lab coat, and he wheeled out a machine that looked like it had come out of Frankenstein's castle. He told the crowd he would contact the Count with his new invention, "The Manolescolator," and soon the machine was buzzing with sparks flying and a series of lights flashing in sequence. Then the eerie voice of the Count from beyond the grave yelled, "Rrrr- rrrock and roll!"

Leas started the familiar drum beat and we tore into "Whip it." At one point we all joined at the same mic to sing "I said whip it. Whip it good!" After a long instrumental jam the song ended with Manolesco's booming voice: "The experiment—is a SUCCESS!"

There was a slight pause, and suddenly the audience broke out into a loud sustained applause. Manolesco's dream of performing "Whip It" on stage with the No-Counts had finally came true, twenty-two years after his death.

People came up to congratulate us as we all headed to the bar for a victory drink, and a guy grabbed me to say how much he enjoyed the performance. He was with the Booji Boy Archives, Devo's official historians, and had videotaped the performance for posterity. He told me he was with Mark Mothersbaugh a few years earlier when my request for a testimonial arrived. They listened to the tape, and Mothersbaugh said it really creeped him out.

Manolesco would have been deeply honored.

"Shooting pool with a rope!"

Night Shift Guy in an Alternate Universe

HIS NAME WAS FLOYD Andrew Boggs, but everyone just called him "Boggs." He would feed information to Art Fantroy and Dave Baron, WERE's traffic copter pilots, and that was a job that he did pretty well. He also had just enough imagination to make him dangerous.

Boggs' career path was like performance art. When he first started out he worked a split shift, morning and afternoon drive, meaning you were there 5–9 a.m. and then from 3–7 p.m. with a six-hour break between. Talk about a lunch hour! He also landed an overnight gig doing news and trading off-color stories with "Stoney" Stoneman at WOBL—or as it was better known, "Wobble" radio—in Oberlin. That didn't last long because he would take one of the two WERE news cars to his second job, leaving the other one for the rest of the staff to share. Management found out and took the keys, and no transportation meant no WOBL for Boggs.

Boggs was like Woody Allen's Broadway Danny Rose. Everyone had a favorite story.

In 1978, WERE held a lavish party at the Hollenden House Hotel to thank its clients and drum up new business. The entire staff was required to show in rented tuxes, and spouses were expected in formal attire as well. Boggs was invited, but none of his usual dates could make it. He didn't want to go "stag," so he decided to hire an "escort" from a "service" he found in the phone book. When Boggs arrived it was like the dinner party scene from the film *Borat*. His date was dressed for a typical night on the job, and Boggs probably didn't realize that he'd paid her for more than just hanging onto his arm and loading up on free booze and fancy food.

The next year, the station was running on fumes and switched from all news to a news and talk format. The owners had a well deserved reputation for cutting expenses, but most on the staff just called them cheap, and the 1979 staff Christmas party was a prime example. It was open only to the staff in the conference room, no guests, and consisted of a few bottles of out-of-state liquor and a bowl of Twix candy bars. The future was far from bright, and the mood was like a birthday party for someone who was terminally ill. People laughed too loud at jokes that weren't funny while wondering where their next job would be. In retrospect, you would be hard pressed to even call it a party. It was more like a support group. Then Boggs entered the room.

The code of the media is, "If it's free, take three." Media folks are notorious for having their hands out, and if it's an open bar you may as well serve it in a trough for everyone to dip their heads into. In Boggs' defense it's likely he didn't have much experience with hard liquor, and that's not something you jump into head first. But with few options, Boggs started to drink his share and more. Before long he was very drunk, and a long night had begun.

Don Robertson was the long-time columnist at the *Cleveland Press* and a veteran radio and TV talk show host. He did an early-evening show at WERE and would buzz the newsroom if he needed anything. As the party/wake broke up a little before 7 o'clock, Robertson started buzzing frantically. Folks ran in to see Robertson grappling with Boggs as he tried to get him away from the microphone. Plus, he had to do the station ID and switch over to the network. The audience heard Robertson gasping, "This . . . is . . . Don . . . Robertson . . . the Don Robertson show . . . and . . . now to . . . ABC!"

Boggs, although not a member of AFTRA, the announcers union, had decided to go on the air during Robertson's show.

"Get him out of here!" Robertson yelled.

Now, Boggs was not a big guy. He was maybe five feet tall. But it took three people to lead him out of the studio and into the newsroom. He needed to get home to bed because he had to be on duty early the next morning, but Boggs was in no condition to drive. After several tries, he was able to remember a friend's number, the call was made, and Boggs was told to watch the closed-circuit TV camera by the side door and to buzz in his friend when she arrived.

Don Robertson was assured that everything was under control, but that didn't stop him from giving a play by play of that evening's events on the air. Then, suddenly, a frantic buzzing came out of the newsroom and staff members rushed to see what was going on. Boggs had tears in his eyes and choked out, "There's a little black kid by the door! He won't come in! Somebody's going to jump him!" Problem was, Boggs wasn't looking at the closed circuit TV. He was watching *Different Strokes* on the newsroom TV. He was trying to buzz in the show's star, Gary Coleman!

Eventually, Boggs was on his way home. Everyone at the party had seen what happened. Newsrooms have a dark humor, and wheels started to turn.

The next morning, Boggs came in to the station looking like he had met the business end of a truck. Ray Hoffman was at the editor's desk and loudly asked, "What the hell are you doing here?!"

Boggs didn't know what he was talking about and certainly didn't remember the night before.

Hoffman gave him a concerned look. "You decked Kim Colebrook!" he said. Colebrook was the station's general manager, stood well over six feet, and was built like a linebacker. The whole morning crew joined in to say what an ugly scene it was and that Boggs had better keep a very low profile.

At 9 a.m., Boggs was out the door like a shot. In truth, he and Colebrook had very little chance of crossing paths because of the split shift, but Boggs made it a point to stay out of his way. Oddly enough, no one let Colebrook in on the joke. The next year, the station held another low-rent holiday get together, with both Boggs and Colebrook in attendance. Boggs took a few shots of liquid courage, marched up to Colebrook and loudly apologized for laying him out the year before. Colebrook didn't know what he was talking about, but said, "Andy. It takes a big man to admit his mistakes." Then he turned around with a look that said, "What the . . . ?"

News/talk radio can be very expensive, and if you don't have ratings to sell, budget cuts are inevitable. By 1980, Boggs found himself with a dotted line across his neck. Here's the problem: Boggs had had a rough childhood, and radio was his escape. He truly loved the medium, and nobody wanted to see him lose his job. The management offered him a gig as an overnight board operator. It was an entry level job, so it didn't pay much, but it did have health coverage and kept him off the street. That would keep him going until he found another position. It was not an easy ride for all parties involved.

Boggs would tape news feeds off the network, do some minor production work, and put local commercials—"spots"—in Mutual radio's syndicated Larry King show. He had some mobility problems, but he still had plenty of time after his assigned work. Maybe too much time.

The morning drive crew would start arriving around 4 a.m. to be on the air at 5:30. In the hour between their arrival and Boggs' heading out at 5, they would hear his wild tales about the bizarre street people on Chester Avenue, the trials and tribulations of his daily life, and his romantic exploits. Especially his romantic life. Boggs got around and had a series of affairs with single and married women. He just looked for women who were free during his off hours. The morning guys would listen to his stories, sometimes in disgust, and try to convince him to slow down.

Ken Prewitt tried to explain it in terms of the zero-sum principle: You only have so many resources to draw on, and when they're gone, that's it. "One day, you're shooting pool with a rope!" Prewitt told him. It all went over Boggs' head.

The job could get a little hectic at times. Boggs had to tape the overnight weather forecast by a certain hour and record network feeds at the same time. He would occasionally get a call from one of his "friends" and would forget the tape was rolling. The call would be on the feed tape, and occasionally Casey Coleman

Andy Boggs finally got to meet the guy whose show he kept on the air at WERE, Larry King. The most interesting thing about this photo is that it was snapped by actor McLean Stevenson. Boggs asked him to take the picture as he was passing by. *Courtesy of Andy Boggs*

would get a morning eye-opener when he reviewed the tape for his sportscast.

Boggs would work on his own projects in the air studio between spot breaks, and would often leave them behind after his shift. He left behind song lyrics, prose, and stories he wrote about his life. There was even an autobiographical play and an outline for a late night comedy show like *Saturday Night Live* that he called *Andy and Company*. ("Some people are calling their friends. Others are calling their lawyers. It's Andy and Company.")

*   *   *

A personal note from Mike: December 1980 was also memorable for a different and far more tragic reason. At that time I was the morning editor at WERE and woke up at 2:45 every morning to get to work by 4 a.m. That meant I hit the hay by 9 p.m. at the latest. Andy Oeftering, the former WERE reporter who had moved on to New York, called me at home at midnight to tell me John Lennon had been gunned down outside the Dakota. It would be the only thing anyone would be talking about the next day, and I decided to head in to the station early. I called Boggs to tell him to roll tape on any John Lennon interviews, news reports from New York, Beatles music, anything. We would need it through the morning.

"Fine," Boggs said. "Did you hear what happened?"

"No, I'm calling on a hunch!"

I walked into the station about a half an hour later.

Midnight was a busy time for Boggs, and every night at the witching hour he had a lot on his plate. He had left a message for Jane Scott at the *Plain Dealer* and that's when she called in. Midnight. Folks in radio will remember that you had to properly erase tapes with a magnetic degausser, and it had to be done evenly or there would be an audible "whoop" every few seconds on the tape. Boggs told me as I walked in that he'd gotten an interview with Scott, who had covered the Beatles during their Cleveland visits. Alleluia! He saved the day! We had tape for our lead stories. I sat down to listen to the tapes and every few seconds, you guessed it: *whoop, whoop, whoop.*

I put my head down and started banging my fist on the desk. Boggs, sensing something was wrong, started banging his fist along with mine in sequence. I can't help but that think that if some alien race was monitoring us from space they would have thought it was some type of weird ritual dance. Boggs knew I was upset, and that made him extremely agitated. This was not a time to fall apart, so I told him to call our morning reporter, Obie Shelton, and tell him Lennon had been shot to death in New York and to come in right away.

When Boggs got excited, he would talk at a hundred miles an hour and often didn't take care to enunciate properly. What Obie heard was that *Leonard* had been killed. That was the name of the program director! Obie later told me that he was wiping away tears in the shower, thinking, "This guy had kids! What a tragedy!" But as he drove in he heard the news updates, figured out what had happened, and came in shooting daggers from his eyes at Boggs.

In the media you get a thick skin to all the tragedy, and humor is a way to relieve tension. It's when you're alone that the severity of a situation will hit you.

WERE had a public address system that was linked to a phone extension. You could dial a certain extension, be connected to the PA, and be heard through the entire station. You could also dial extensions after calling the main number from outside the station after hours. A bunch of folks from the station got together for a party one Friday night and, after a few cocktails, wondered if you could reach the PA extension through the switchboard. The only folks at the WERE building after midnight were Boggs and the WGCL jock, who stayed in the studio. Every ten minutes someone would call in to the PA extension and whisper into the phone. *"Boggs. I'm in the building. I'm watching you. I'm behind the door, Boggs. Can you see me? Coming to get you, buddy!"*

I had to leave the party early because I had a Saturday morning air shift, so I'm not sure how long the calls went on. I just know that I walked in at 4 a.m., said "Hello Boggs," and he jumped five feet in the air, his eyes bugging out like ping-pong balls.

*   *   *

The staff was constantly reminded that the stations were strapped for cash and everyone had to keep a lid on expenses. Nobody bought much of what the management said anyway. The staff had nicknames for many members of the management, including "Fats," "Iscariot" or "the Dead Guy," "Moose and Squirrel," and "the Man with Three Buttocks." At one point the owner of the station suggested the newsroom use both sides of the wire copy from Associated Press and United Press International. That, of course, was impossible because each story was torn off individually for the studio and they would have to be taped together to be fed back into the machine.

Eventually, it was determined that Boggs' salary and benefits were too costly and had to be cut in favor of a part-timer. Boggs had been there a long time, and no one wanted to see him lose his job.

Boggs lived at the Carter Manor, the old Pick-Carter Hotel (now public housing), and it was suggested we could afford to keep him if he gave up the apartment and moved into the station. He could set up a cot in the boiler room, there was a microwave and refrigerator in the newsroom, there were plenty of TVs and a shower in the upstairs men's room. The boiler room was fairly private. The only time anyone went in there was to fix something, or a staff member from WERE or WGCL would sneak off to smoke weed or drink old bottles of cheap "People Power" wine (often during their air shifts!) that had been stashed there. Plus, Boggs wouldn't have to pay for utilities or phone and could be on 24-hour call. On the other hand, this would violate housing codes. And then there was Boggs' very active "social life." The idea was shot down before it was even presented to management. As it turned out, Boggs was able to juggle some numbers, get some help from government grants, and clean out his bank account to buy a double house on the near west side of Cleveland for income property. He rented out the two housing units and moved into the basement.

Even so, you couldn't stop the inevitable. Boggs got his notice, and the staff took him to a restaurant for a sendoff. He was also given a couple of bottles of expensive wine that didn't see the next morning. Boggs would go on to earn his bachelor's degree, start his own web site, and write his online autobiography—with a different story line than most would remember.

"You're never going to make it in this business!"

Local Radio Legends from Earlier Days

WGAR HAD A LONG history before John Lanigan started there in December 1971. Guys like Joe Mayer, Phil Gardner, Fig Newton, "Real Bob" James, and others kept AM radio alive and kicking during the transition to FM, and that's because they were all top-notch entertainers. The formula for success was simple: Make every show, no matter what part of the day, sound like morning drive. That meant lots of prep and plenty of energy. Plus, all the jocks had those special personalities that made their shows unique. Gardner and Newton had that dry, Tim Conway type of humor and knew how to pull it off. James had a rapid-fire delivery with a lot of produced bits and, because 'GAR was a 50,000-watt blowtorch, he fed a huge audience across the country. Every night there would be calls from dozens of locations across the U.S. in his "Parade of States."

But make no mistake, the big dog on the block was Lanigan. Lanigan had a razor-sharp sense of humor, and he made you want to get out of bed every morning so you wouldn't miss anything. He also knew how to get the best out of his listeners. His "Flex Club" quizzed callers about their first time and where they "flexed" in public. (Try to tell me you don't know what that means!) Lanigan worked constantly, hosting WUAB's midday movie, doing appearances and performing in clubs at night. He even had his own nightclub for a time at the Eastgate Shopping Center in Mayfield.

Lanigan was and is a very funny man, but he made no secret of the fact that he also used radio comedy services and freelance writers. If it was entertaining, it got on the air. But most would say the best part of the day was total improvisation. That's when he handed the show off to Joe Mayer at 10 a.m.

Mayer was already a legend when he took the job at WGAR. He was "Emperor Mayer" during WHK's Top 40 years in the 1960s, and managed bands like The Grasshoppers with guitarist "Ben Eleven Letters." Of course, that was his stage name. His real last name was Orzechowski, and he became Ben Orr when he joined the Cars a few years later. Mayer was the perfect straight man to Lanigan, and their five minutes every day was "must hear" radio. People loved Joe Mayer, and he was even being courted by WMJI years after he retired. When Mayer died in 1997, Congressman Dennis Kucinich honored him with a special salute at the Capitol. Kucinich is quoted in the Congressional Record of June 5, 1997:

> Mr. Speaker, I rise to honor the memory of Joe Mayer, whose radio show and personality were known to many admirers in Cleveland, the rock 'n' roll capital of America. Joe was born in Cleveland and went to high school in Fairview Park. He served in the U.S. Navy as a radioman during World War II. Joe's radio career spanned more than 34 years. He made his debut in 1953 at WEOL in Elyria. He grew in popularity along with rock 'n' roll at stations WHK and WGAR. When the Beatles came to Cleveland in 1964, Joe put them up in his home. He was master of ceremonies for the Rolling Stones' first Cleveland concert. Joe and rock 'n' roll were bound together in Cleveland's music consciousness.
>
> His voice, energy, and personality will be greatly missed.

Okay, that part about the Beatles was urban legend. It just wasn't true. But you see how well loved the guy was.

The "Friendly Station" had a long history of notable personalities. A lot of people forget that Jack Paar worked at WGAR. Even sadder, a lot of people have forgotten Jack Paar! He redefined late-night TV talk shows when he took over *The Tonight Show* from

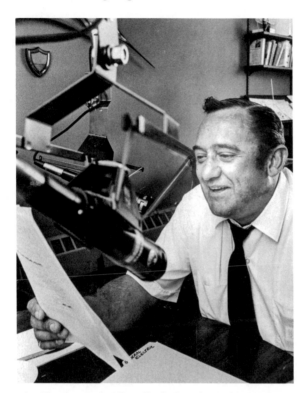

Joe Mayer was a longtime disc jockey whose career took a new turn when he started trading jokes with John Lanigan at WGAR in the 1970s. *Cleveland Press Collection, Cleveland State University Archives*

Steve Allen and before handing it off to Johnny Carson. But like a lot of folks he started out dreaming of a broadcasting career, and that dream took off in Cleveland.

Paar was born in Canton, moved to Michigan, and faced a lot of adversity. He overcame a stuttering problem and battled tuberculosis. That didn't stop his passion for radio, and as a teenager he took whatever jobs he could get at small stations just to get his foot in the door. He was still a kid when his family moved back to the Cleveland area and Paar landed the gig at WGAR.

It wasn't much of a job, and it certainly wasn't glamorous. A lot of it was behind the scenes, but Paar had a strong radio voice and even got a chance to do a little air work now and then. Then, something happened in 1938 that would change Paar's life forever. Paar told the story to David Letterman in 1986.

Paar had been at WGAR for a few years, but still had the lowest seniority and that meant the worst shifts. He was also the youngest announcer in the U.S. That meant nothing to the management. He had to prove himself. Paar worked Sunday nights, and when he started out his dad would drop him off at the trolley line for the trip to downtown Cleveland. Like a lot of teenagers, he spent his money on clothes, graduating from knickers to smart business suits. Those were also the days when you dressed for success and business attire was required on all shifts. Paar showed up for work for his Sunday shift, did the news and station ID ("WGAR, Cleveland. Bulova watch time, 8 p.m.") and called his mom to ask how he sounded. She assured him he sounded great.

Now it was time for the moment that made Sunday nights special. Cleveland was an exciting place, and people were everywhere, even on a Sunday night. There were plenty of restaurants downtown, and Paar would treat himself to a club sandwich and a malted milk. On that October night, he ran out to the deli, got his evening meal to go, and brought it back to the station. There was an engineer on duty, and the Mercury Theater was on the air. About five minutes into the show, Paar sat down in the announcer's booth for an easy night ahead. As it turned out, easy was not in the cards.

Paar wasn't listening to the show. He had a sandwich to eat, and he wasn't needed until the network break. WGAR had eight phone lines. They called them trunk lines, and along with doing the news it was Paar's job to answer the phones. Sundays were usually a pretty easy night. But this was not a usual night.

The phone rang, Paar swallowed that first bite and answered the line. "That bulletin! People are landing in New Jersey! What's happening? What are we going to do?!"

Soon every line was lit, with one panicked call after another. Paar didn't realize it was Orson Welles' updated version of H.G.

Jack Paar was the nation's youngest radio announcer when he started out at WGAR. He's seen here interviewing film great George Raft.

Wells' *War of the Worlds*, and he didn't have time to find out more. The phones were going crazy! He tried to reassure everyone that it was only a drama. At least he was pretty sure it was only a drama. It was time for Paar to make a call.

Pat Patterson was the station manager, and had his doubts about Paar. His phone rang, and Paar blurted out "Hell's breaking loose here, Mr. Pat! I think there's trouble in New Jersey!"

This is not the way Patterson wanted to end his weekend. He told Paar, "You're much too emotional—and you're never going to make it!" But he did say he would make some calls to see what was happening.

Meanwhile, Paar had to deal with the phones at WGAR, and the calls kept coming in, each one more desperate than the last. Paar couldn't take it any longer and decided to take action. There was a red kill switch in the announcer's booth that would cut the network feed, and he hit the button to go back to local programming. He cracked the mike open to say, "Ladies and gentlemen, this is a drama—I think. We're checking with New Jersey. Please don't call the station. I can't take any more of this! But be calm! Be calm!"

Cleveland didn't hear the entire broadcast of *The War of the Worlds* because of the youngest announcer in America.

That didn't sit well with Mr. Pat. He was listening at home and wasn't about to let a twenty-year-old make programming decisions. There was an angry phone call, and he told Paar to be in his office first thing the next morning. Jack Paar would soon be looking for a new station. At least that was the plan.

On Monday, the elevator door opened on the penthouse floor of the Statler Hotel, Paar stepped out—and was blinded by flash bulbs! He was a hero! He was billed as the "kid who calmed Cleveland!" Pat Patterson didn't have much of a choice. Paar stayed on the payroll.

There wasn't a lot of turnover at WGAR. It was a prime gig, and people stayed as long as they could. Paar was slow to move up the totem pole. In December 1941 he was still doing Sundays, now in the afternoon, and still getting his usual malted milk and club sandwich. As he unwrapped his sandwich, he could hear the network talking about some place called Pearl Harbor. What was Pearl Harbor? This can't be true. They're doing it again—at least that's what he thought in the beginning. But the more he listened, the more legitimate it sounded and, sure enough, the phones were on fire. Time for a call to Mr. Pat.

Patterson didn't want to talk to Paar. "You again! You're never going to make it! Now what's happening?"

"They say they're bombing some place called Pearl Harbor."

Patterson made it clear. "You are not to press that button and take us off CBS! If there's World War II, I don't want you involved." But Paar did get involved. Like a lot of Americans he signed up for service and saw action at Guadalcanal before continuing his career and making TV history.

Ray Kozlowski would make history in a different way.

The news business was a lot different in the Fifties and Sixties.

Newspapers and radio fought for audience, and for guys in the news business, TV was the last stop before you took a job in a shoe store. That would start to change with the JFK assassination, but prior to that people saw it this way: the papers had depth, and radio had immediacy. TV was an also-ran. The reporters were different, too. Today you would call it "old school." It was like that movie *The Front Page*—fast-talking characters with their ties loosened and a press pass in the hatband of their fedoras. There was a lot of competition and a lot of pressure to get the story first. Most reporters were heavy smokers, and they could sure knock back the drinks. You fought tooth and nail to get a story before another reporter, and a few hours later you'd bend an elbow with the same guy, laughing and closing the bar at the Press Club. Ray Kozlowski felt very comfortable in that world.

Kozlowski grew up in the city and after he graduated from Western Reserve University, he found himself reporting for the *Cleveland News,* one of the city's three daily papers. When the *News* went belly up in 1960, Kozlowski was able to land a gig at WGAR. They had a top-notch news staff, and Kozlowski hit the ground running. Every day was an adventure. He could cover President Kennedy one day and a grisly murder the next. Kozlowski was even strapped into an electric chair at the Ohio Penitentiary for a documentary on capital punishment. You had to have a pretty thick skin when you worked in news, but you could have some fun.

WGAR had Kozlowski riding an ostrich against Ray Stawriaski, WJW-TV's "Franz the Toymaker." He faced off in a radio/TV hockey game against Bob "Hoolihan" Wells, Ron Penfound ("Captain Penny") and others at the Cleveland Arena. Other days were just boring. That's the way it was on Thursday, October 15, 1964. But that would change quickly.

The Yankees and Cardinals were battling it out in St. Louis in game seven of the World Series, and WGAR carried the game. That meant no newscasts, so Kozlowski just spent that part of the afternoon chasing down stories. To break the monotony, he decided to call an old friend at Reuters news agency in Paris. They chatted for awhile and out of nowhere, Kozlowski's friend was interrupted. "What? Khrushchev's deposed?! How did that happen? Who's in charge? Ray, I have to go." In the midst of the Cold War, Ray had just overheard the story of a lifetime. He checked to see if any of the wires had anything and came up blank. At 2:15, the Yankees' Elston Howard was on first base and Cards pitcher Bob Gibson was on the mound when Kozlowski cut the network programming for a special report. Fellow anchor George Engle introduced him: "We interrupt this program to bring you special bulletin from the WGAR newsroom. Here's Ray Kozlowski."

Kozlowski announced:

Very reliable sources inform WGAR news this afternoon that Premier Khrushchev has been removed as the top man in the Soviet Union. The source said that Undersecretary of State George Ball was to be in Cleveland this afternoon for a news conference but had been ordered to call Washington when he was about 100 miles out of Cleveland. Although the sources are reliable, there has been no confirmation from the Soviet Union. For other details, here is George Engle.

Engle picked it up from there:

The speculation of a change in the upper echelons of the Kremlin was prompted by an earlier report that *Isvestia*, the Soviet government newspaper, did something unusual, announcing it would not publish an edition tonight. Such action usually means major Kremlin developments are in the works. But western observers are not commenting officially on what might be coming up, if anything. A London newspaper, the *Evening News*, reported there were signs in Moscow of government changes which could affect Khrushchev. Speculation has been heightened by Khrushchev's absence from the public scene for the last few days. Yesterday, the Soviet news agency Tass said Khrushchev was vacationing at his home in the Crimea resort. A fleet of black limousines was seen yesterday and today outside the Communist party Central Committee headquarters building indicating that the all powerful group was meeting but they're meeting in secret. It was at a Central Committee meeting that Khrushchev rose to sole leadership of Russia back in 1957.

Western communist correspondents in Moscow were alerted to stand by to await an important announcement on the Soviet radio tonight. What that announcement might be has not been definitely ascertained by anyone yet, but we'll repeat the bulletin broadcast by Ray Kozlowski moments ago. Very reliable sources informing WGAR news that Premier Khrushchev has been removed as the top man in the Soviet Union. This speculation heightened by the fact that Undersecretary of State George Ball was to be in Cleveland at 2:30 this afternoon for a news conference, but had been ordered to call Washington when he was about a hundred miles out of Cleveland. Although the sources that inform WGAR news are reliable, there is no official confirmation from the Soviet Union or the United States State Department as yet. We return you now to the World Series baseball game.

Ray Kozlowski had just broken a story of worldwide importance on WGAR in Cleveland—nearly 5,000 miles away from the Kremlin! It was very likely that the countries of the Soviet Union had yet to hear the story, but a reporter in Northeast Ohio put it on the air before any other news outlet. It wasn't long before the news started trickling out of Moscow. Sure enough, Khrushchev had "voluntarily" retired, with Leonid Brezhnev and Alexei Kosygin moving in to assume power.

No one was sure how he did it, but Ray Kozlowski had come through, big time, and there was plenty of congratulations and back-slapping to go around. Tom O'Brien was director of radio news for ABC, and he wrote to 'GAR's news director Engle to say, "Next time you get anything like this, beating out all the major wire

A worldwide scoop! WGAR's Ray Kozlowski broke the story that Nikita Khrushchev had been deposed — even before they heard the news in Moscow.

services and radio networks, remember our telephone number!" That was high praise because WGAR was not an ABC affiliate at the time. Congressman Michael Feighan wrote to say, "It is certainly not very often that a story of such international interest originates in Moscow and is broken in Cleveland. I am sure your superiors are proud to have a man like you on their staff." By all accounts, they were.

The station kept Ray Kozlowski busy. On Mother's Day 1965 his wife, Dolores, joined with wives of other announcers to take over the station and do their husband's jobs. There was a lot of social change in the mid-Sixties, and Kozlowski covered the riots in Glenville and Hough, and student riots against the Vietnam war. His son, Robert, was a kid at the time, and remembers his dad coming home after a grueling 36-hour shift, tired and unshaven, and complaining about dodging eggs being thrown at police. The egg shells all over his dad's rain coat.

There was change on the radio dial, too.

By 1968, early progressive rock started popping up on the FM band, and WGAR-FM would become "People's Radio," WNCR. Kozlowski didn't like the music, the lifestyle, or the jocks. He'd complain, "The music stinks, and you can't understand the lyrics! What are they trying to say?! 'Up, up and away in my beautiful balloo'—what the hell is a balloo?" (It was obviously the Fifth Dimension singing about a hot air *balloon*, but radio people are notorious for damaged hearing.) Or, "These kids spinning the records—Ginger Sutton? Who the hell names their kid Ginger?!" Ginger was the name Steve Sinton used for radio. He would go on to long, successful careers in both media and politics but, granted, some of the guys who worked at WNCR could be a little unsettling to the older generation.

The radio industry was always very competitive. Kozlowski eventually parted ways with WGAR, and found that his past success didn't hold much water when he started looking for another job.

He slowed down a bit, working smaller stations now and then and getting more involved around his hometown in Garfield Heights. He worked on some political campaigns, and was even the field announcer for events at Garfield Heights High. Still, life wasn't the same, and Kozlowski felt the pressure. His marriage to Dolores came to an end, he moved in with his parents in Euclid, and starting spending a lot more time with the bottle. A lot of radio people will tell you they went through the same thing. For a time he even lived in his car, and eventually checked in to the Stella Maris treatment center for help. It was too late. Ray Kozlowski died far too young at the rehab center. His son Robert would later hear that police found his dad's abandoned car, and it was towed to a junk yard for demolition. The back seat was packed to the roof with mementoes of his career at WGAR.

"You stay in that world and you'll be a bum and a roustabout!"

Milton Maltz Creates a Broadcast Dynasty

MOST PEOPLE OUTSIDE THE business look at radio for news and entertainment, but before computers and the digital age came along, it had a completely different role. Radio, especially in Northeast Ohio, was lifestyle. Your favorite station reflected your views and your taste in entertainment, as well as being your source for breaking news. It set trends and brought people together, and the station you listened to told a lot about you as a person.

Cleveland had some of the most creative and competitive stations in the country, and starting in the mid-1970s, WMMS laid the groundwork for a broadcast dynasty. The station grew at a rapid pace and would eventually win ratings books that disabled the other stations. It had a massive, loyal audience. But the Buzzard, as it was known, had its critics, too—mostly from other stations that couldn't compete or broadcasters who couldn't get a gig there. If you don't get invited to the party, chances are you'll tell everyone that the party sucked.

By the 1980s, WMMS was a juggernaut that gobbled up the competition and spit it out, leaving any station that dared to challenge it to pick up the pieces. Station executives came and went, and stations changed formats, but anyone who was named to program against the Buzzard would find out in short order that they were on a career path that could be likened to a suicide mission. WMMS was the perfect storm, and its owner Milton Maltz was the god of thunder.

There was a joke back then that asked the question, "What do Milt Maltz's employees call him behind his back?" Answer: "Mr. Maltz." This was a guy who wanted you to call him by his first name, but he cast a long shadow and most didn't feel comfortable being so informal. At the Statler Office Tower, Maltz's office was down the hall from the production, programming, and news departments. If you wanted a conversation, you could look down the hallway and, if his door was open, just walk right in. If the door was closed, you asked for an appointment.

When you landed at WMMS, you knew you were at the top. Plenty tried and few made the cut, and you never wanted for anything. If you needed something in order to do your job, it was overnighted. If you had an idea, they backed you. A major concert in London? WMMS sent a crew. Someone recording in New York? See if you can get an interview. The station booked airfare and rooms and reimbursed for any other expenses.

You knew this was the best job you were ever going to have, so when the management suggested it needed something done, no matter how difficult, you were too proud to say you couldn't do it. It was also in the back of your head that there were plenty of folks lined up to take your place if you failed, so you did your best to do the impossible. Lots of people became very motivated!

Staff meetings could be like tent revivals. They were often loud and raucous with an energy focused on one thing: destroying the competition. A lot of that energy was centered on the soft-spoken guy who carried a big stick, but it's unlikely that Milton Maltz ever foresaw himself standing in front of his army in Cleveland or even in radio. It all started with *Moby Dick*.

Let's turn back the clock a few years. Fourteen-year old Milton Maltz was in a Chicago classroom, and his teacher had all the students read a passage from *Moby Dick* aloud.

"Her name was Mrs. Clausen, and I'll never forget her as long as I live," Maltz recalls. "She said, 'Milton, I want you to stay after class.' Oh hell, what did I do wrong? She said, 'Downtown at WBEZ they're starting a new show called Radio Make Believe.' So what's that got to do with me? She said, 'The first one is 'Jack and the Beanstalk', and you can be Jack!' Why? I'm no actor. She said, 'But you can pass that audition. I know you can!' I didn't think so, but she said she would pay my carfare. I was still agonizing over what I wanted to be. Maybe an architect. Then she said, 'When you're standing there in the hall as a hall monitor, you're bored, aren't you?' Yeah, I was. 'I'll get you off of that!' So I went downtown for the audition, and the next thing I know it's 'Fee-Fi-Fo-Fum! I smell the blood of an Englishman!', and I'm on the radio. They started calling me for other parts. My father warned me, 'You stay in that world and you'll be a bum and a roustabout!'"

Maltz's training as a kid actor lit a spark. Like many before him, he joined the military. He moonlighted in his free time at a local station. That's where he met John Kluge, who would play a huge role in his journey into radio.

"When I was in the Navy, I was attached to the National Security Agency in Washington, D.C.," Maltz recalled. "I was through at 4:15 every afternoon and I would get in my old Chevrolet. During the day I was a GI, and at night I was a DJ in Washington, working for John at his first radio station. We got to know each other real well, and he thought, 'This looks like an interesting business.' He was in the grocery wholesale business, and he thought, 'Maybe I should buy more stations.' We would talk for several hours at a time, and when I got out of the Navy I left Washington to go back to broadcasting as I knew it."

Maltz's interest in radio went beyond the air studio. It started back when he was a kid actor, and it centered on three main elements that would guide his career as a station owner.

"First of all, you have to have the technology with a strong signal. I've always been involved with improving the signals of the stations. There I am at this station doing the shows, and I went to the engineer, a guy named Andriesen, and I said, How does this signal, how does this stuff go on the radio? He said, 'The tower,' and I asked, Where's the tower? 'Atop the Morrison Hotel.' Can I go up there with you when you fix it? When you work on it? 'Of course!'

So I went up there with him and began to learn about the technical side. I also started reading books on allocations of frequencies."

Step number two is programming. That's simple enough: Give the audience something to listen to that will keep them coming back for more.

Then the final element, which includes the guys in suits in sales, administration and marketing.

"How many people that I came across were knowledgeable in all three?" Maltz says. "Not many. Either they're programmers, they're engineers or they are sales or marketing people. That's the difference in finding stations that are in trouble, because they need to be fixed. If you have one or two of those, and if you're lucky, all three of those are bad and you can get them cheap."

But in the 1950s and '60s, Maltz also had faith in one area of broadcasting that was pretty much ignored by most: FM radio, which at the time was impressing no one. Better sound, no static—FM should have been the place to be, right?

"Where was FM back in the '50s and '60s?" Maltz asks. "It was in the 40 megahertz band. It wasn't where it is today. How did it get moved? I have my own philosophy. Every major 50,000-watt clear channel was owned by people who didn't want to see FM happen. It was going to take away audience. It had fidelity that AM did not. Somehow or other the FCC changed it so all the frequencies were moved off. If you recall, you didn't buy an AM/FM radio. You bought either an AM or an FM, and now if you had an old FM radio it was obsolete. It didn't pick up anything. It was moved to where it is today. It set back FM broadcasting at least two decades."

But there were plenty of FM signals to be had, and Maltz saw the potential.

By the 1960s, Maltz had formed Malrite Communications Group, a bunch of small market stations based in Mt. Clemens, Michigan. In 1972 he bought a station in San Diego, which presented a golden opportunity. His wife, Tamar, had family that had relocated to the west coast from Chicago.

"San Diego, Santa Monica, L.A.—she was so delighted I bought this station in San Diego. We're out there for the closing. It was a 50,000-watt AM and a decent FM. The owner said, 'You know, nobody wants FM. It stands for free music, so I'm going to keep the FM. You buy the AM.' Uh-oh. Maltz believed FM was the future and said, "That's not the deal we made! The FM goes with the AM or I'm out of here!"

The deal fell apart. Things would turn around quickly just a few days later. It happened at the National Association of Broadcasters Convention at the Stevens Hotel in Chicago.

Maltz was buying a paper at a newsstand when he met up with his old friend, John Kluge, now the head of Metromedia Broadcasting. Kluge confirmed a rumor that he'd just bought a station in Dallas—his eighth, meaning he'd have to sell one, per the law at the time. Maltz asked which one. "Probably Cleveland," Kluge replied, and then suggested that Maltz buy it. "You can really fix it!" Within 15 minutes they shook hands on the deal.

"I had to now go home and say to Tamar, my wife, that we have a broadcast deal. There's one little problem—it's not San Diego. It's Cleveland, Ohio!"

At first the couple stayed in Chicago. "The worst part was, when I finally found a house here, in Shaker Heights, she wouldn't come. So I was on Wright Airlines every day from Chicago back and forth, and I was getting sick of it. I said, 'We gotta move,' so she finally comes to look at the house, and what's the headline in the local paper? The president had called a big meeting in Washington of all the mayors of major cities, and Mayor Perk had to turn it down. Why? It was his wife's bowling night! My wife asked, 'What kind of a town are you taking me to?!'

"Today she loves the city, and she doesn't call it Cleveland. She calls it, 'My beloved Cleveland!'"

So Malrite took over WHK-AM and WMMS-FM. Those were the days when AM was still the moneymaker.

"When I bought the station, WHK was *the* station, obviously," Maltz said. "The FM had thirty or forty thousand dollars a year income. Total! It was in the hole and I said to the sales manager

'We've got to go out and make some calls together.' He said, 'I can handle it all!' 'No, no, no. I'm sure you can but I want to go with you.'"

They started with the local Pepsi-Cola distributor.

"The woman who handled the account at the agency said, 'I haven't seen you in six months! How are you? What's up?'" Maltz recalls. "I knew right then there was trouble. When we left, we were using his car. I had seen awards in his office for winning local golf tournaments. I said, 'Do me a favor. Open up your trunk.'" There were golf clubs. Maltz picked up the golf clubs and smelled them. Fresh grass. "I asked him, 'What the hell are you trying to do? You got a job. You want it or not?' He said, 'You got me.' That meant I had to go out and get a new sales manager."

Then there were some restless hippies at WMMS.

These were the days of the so-called "generation gap." The old saying was, "Don't trust anyone over 30," and WMMS was the voice of the counter-culture. It was time for the troops to meet the new boss. Keep in mind that the hippie mentality was against capitalism and most forms of authority. Underground newspapers like Cleveland's *Great Swamp Erie da da Boom* embraced the music scene but railed against the promoters staging the shows. Life was good if you found someone else to pay for it, and if someone could afford to buy a radio station they were obviously part of the "establishment."

Maltz met with the staff and didn't pull any punches. "I'll tell you what I'm going to do. I'm going to give it one year, and then we'll reassess. I have a second format already booted up if I need it."

Some stepped forward to say they wanted a chance to run the station. They knew the format inside and out and thought they should be in charge. "I looked at them and said, 'You might be right. Tell you what I'll do. I'll put you on probation. Take the job and see how you like it. Let's see how you do, and we'll have a chance to talk to each other periodically."

They would still be managing a business, and one individual

found there was too much administration and working with sales for his liking. His tenure didn't last long; he resigned. Maltz took the risk, but wanted that individual to find out for himself.

Now, how to motivate a group that had just seen its very vocal leader opt out?

"I told them why I was keeping them," Maltz said. "I told them I didn't want smooth-voiced announcers. That belongs on NBC coast to coast, the Lux Radio Theater. I'm renting your brains and your heart. You have it. Don't be afraid to use it. Be yourselves. That's what his station is all about. They loved to hear that."

They also saw what a hands-on owner does when confronted with a problem. The stations were located at 5000 Euclid Avenue at that time. Maltz says, "I came from downstairs only a few weeks later and the toilet was over-running. Water was in the hall and they were all standing around looking at it and didn't know what the hell to do. I went and got a broom and a mop and I started to clean it all up. They all started to laugh and helped me."

The wall was starting to come down, but another incident helped bring around the audience, too.

The sales people were having a hard time selling FM. There were only so many head shops, record stores, and leather places, and they weren't spending a lot of money on advertising. Sure, they played the station in their stores, but that was free. Advertising was not. The stations needed money. Yet they also weren't afraid to turn money down—and that worked in their favor.

"The Vietnam war was on, and I didn't want to take the U.S. Army's commercials," Maltz says. "We needed the money badly, but I turned it down. By the same token, I called the *Plain Dealer*'s radio-TV writer, Bill Hickey, and told him 'This is the only station that doesn't want that business.' He said, 'You mean you're not taking it?!' 'Of course not.' They ran a big story: 'WMMS refuses!' The staff was phenomenal. They were talking it up on the air."

You couldn't buy that kind of credibility.

Other pieces quickly began to fall in place. Maltz recalls one key turning point.

WE DON'T GO TO WORK WE GO TO WAR!

The slogan that drove the Malrite Broadcasting machine. That's Milton Maltz, front right, popping out of the tank.

"David Helton designed the buzzard. We needed a logo, and he came up with an ugly, ugly bird. That was the beginning of the buzzard, and he modified it as time went on. Little by little it began to take off."

Helton's buzzard would become Cleveland's version of Mickey Mouse and would symbolize the WMMS lifestyle as well as the city.

Some key people signed on for long stays as well.

"John Chaffee was of tremendous help. John was the guy who loved this music as much as anybody I'd ever met. You have to remember that in those days we owned a station in Rochester, New York, in Mount Clemens, Michigan, in Minneapolis-St. Paul and Milwaukee, Wisconsin. WMMS was the major station, but it wasn't the only station. It was very important. We also had a good opportunity to meet with our friends in marketing and promotions, the record promoters here and Belkin Productions, the best bookers of all time as far as I'm concerned."

There was also a harmonic convergence of up-and-coming talent that was starting to break along with the station's growth. In 1975, Maltz remembers, "Kid Leo had a young man on the air and was taking him out to the elevator at the old building [at 5000 Euclid Avenue]. I had to give Leo something and I remember coming up to him at the elevator saying, 'Leo, you forgot this.' He said thanks and 'By the way, I want you to meet Bruce Springsteen.' I shook his hand and wished him luck. It was by sheer accident." Most would agree that the guys on both ends of that handshake had a big ride ahead of them.

The station got a lot of Milt Maltz's attention even when he was away from the office.

"I used to listen to the station for how the boys sounded," he says. "I wanted them to be real, I didn't want them to be phony. One Saturday afternoon, I think Kid Leo was on the air or it could have been Matt [Lapczynski]. We're coming from downtown from some event and I said to my wife, 'Something's wrong!' 'What do you mean?' 'I hear strain and stress in his voice.' 'I don't hear anything.' 'That's why I do what I do and you do what you do. We're going to the station.' We go to the station and there's smoke coming out of the control room! There was a small fire. One of the tape recorders was burning. The jock didn't know what the hell to do and he was hoping it would all die out. I said, 'Just turn off all the juice except to keep us on the air and call the fire department.'" Sometimes a calm voice can speak volumes.

Meanwhile, WHK was doing all right, but it was obvious that it could be doing a lot better. There were some personnel changes, some tweaking here and there, but then Maltz caught wind of breaking news down the dial that caused him to take quick and drastic action to one-up the competition. It happened in 1974.

"I heard that WJW-AM was going to go country. WHK was beginning to falter, and I had not paid that much attention to it, but when I heard that WJW was going country, I said I would be back in about an hour. I went in the control room and told Joe Finan, 'We're going to change formats. I'm going downtown to buy records now.' I went to a dime store that had a record department and bought every country western song I could find. I came into the studio and said, 'After the news, we're country!' Joe was absolutely stupefied! He said 'This is absolutely insane! I've never heard of anything like this!' I told him, 'You have now!'"

WJW abandoned plans to go country after WHK beat it to the punch.

The AM air staff had its issues, too. Lots of talent but some pretty big egos, and it didn't stop there. Joe Finan was a good example. He had a history in Cleveland at WERE, but had had a lot of success in the Sixties in Denver. Maltz recalls, "I get a call that there are two policemen in the lobby and they want to arrest Joe. I said 'What?! Send them up here.' They came up and said, 'He's got a stack of violations, traffic tickets, when he went out to Denver and he never paid them, and he hasn't come back and asked for an opportunity to pay them over time.' Let's call Joe in and straighten this out. He was on the air but I had someone else take over for fifteen minutes. He saw the cops and looked scared. I said, 'You're damn right you ought to be scared! We're going to cut a deal now.' We got him off the hook, but he had to figure out how to pay them."

Then there was Gary Dee. Dee pulled in huge numbers down the dial with the "People Power" format, but WERE's sales staff couldn't sell them. As John Chaffee once said, "If you have the number one show in town and you can't sell it, it's not the air talent's fault."

Dee came over to WHK, Don Imus returned to do afternoon drive, Doc Lemon sipped beers and fell asleep live on the air overnight, and WHK fought its sister station for the top of the ratings mountain. Plus, a savvy sales staff and aggressive marketing generated a lot of revenue. Cleveland was now a machine for Maltz, and he had his eyes on a bigger prize.

By the mid-Eighties Milt Maltz was working on other markets, like WHTZ in Newark, New Jersey, which served New York City.

"It had a short tower and was playing foreign language, black music, and anything that could bring in a buck, including trade. Even gasoline for the owners. It had an AM, and I wanted to buy [the FM]. I knew I could move that antenna to the top of the Empire State Building. I took the owners out to dinner at the Pierre Hotel and I offered them a deal. 'You keep the AM, you keep the studios, you keep the real estate. All I want is the FM frequency. I'm offering you $7.3 million.' It's a deal. We shook hands and I called my attorney in Washington and said 'In 24 hours I want a contract ready.'

"Now, how do we get it on top of the Empire State Building? I knew it would work on the FCC side. There was a group of stations already up there. How do you get on their tower?

"The problem was they were all vertically distributing their signals. When you turned a corner you could lose it. The signal distribution looked like a star shape. It wasn't round, and I had an engineer working for me in those days who developed the other side of the antenna. He put together the horizontal and vertical distribution and smoothed out the entire coverage increasing the power. Then I asked for a meeting with all the engineers from all the stations, and I said, 'Here's the latest thing. We tested it on my station at Mt. Clemens, Michigan.' I knew it worked and I gave it a demonstration. They asked, 'How do we do it?' and I said, 'I'll do it for you if you put me on the master antenna.' 'Of course!' That's how we ended up at the top of the Empire State Building. Within seventy-two days we were number one, ages 18 to 34."

Remember the three-piece template? Engineering and marketing were taken care of, but programming in the nation's largest radio market was critical. "Scott Shannon was there from the beginning and we did things differently," according to Maltz. "The agencies that did TV commercials could have also been aired about several other stations in New York. There was no unique quality. Here's what we did. We went on the air and said something that had never been done in broadcasting. We're going to tell the truth. This is the worst station that has ever seen the airwaves in radio

Groundbreaking entertainment. WMMS was well represented when the first shovels hit the dirt for the Rock and Roll Hall of Fame. From left to right: Ed Ferenc, Milton Maltz, Walt Tiburski, Jeff Kinzbach, Laura Farrell. *Brian Chalmers*

in New York. Help us go from worst to first. We had kids crawling up on billboards writing 'From worst to first. Z100.' We called the Empire State building the gorilla building. The print showed King Kong on top."

Engineer Frank Foti adds to that story. He was brought up from Cleveland to help oversee Z100's launch. "I always got the sense of pride Milt Maltz had in WHTZ," he says. "The summer that it went on the air in 1983, Milt Maltz and his wife took a long overdue vacation. They went to Israel, but when they got there word got back that Z100 was ready to go on the air. Mr. Maltz also made the commitment that he was going to take this vacation and would not call back to find out what was going on. But I was in New York and we found out when they were flying back, the fourth of August. Z100 was on the air for its second full day and it was the first day that we got on the air from the Empire State Building.

Station manager Dean Thacker, myself and a couple of other guys got Mr. Maltz's secretary to give us the flight information and we drove out to Kennedy Airport. We were standing just outside of where you would clear customs with a boom box playing Z100 and a t-shirt. Milt Maltz saw us and his eyes were like a little kid on Christmas morning. It was really touching. He came up to Dean and I and asked, "Is it on?!" Yes, Mr. Maltz. 'Frank Foti, is that from the Empire State Building?' Yes sir, it is! He was in a sport coat and tie and he took them off and put on the Z100 t-shirt right there at the airport. He was so happy that we hit the deadline and it was on the air. Malrite had a New York City radio station and 74 days later it went from worst to first."

But Foti also had a deep connection back home at WMMS.

"Dean Thacker and I also knew that at the time the purse strings and spending money was open for us, but there were technical things WMMS needed that they were not getting. So there was stuff that we bought and had shipped to New Jersey, and I would turn it around and ship it to Cleveland. I would call Tom O'Brien and tell him something like 'A harmonizer is going to show up.' For years Tom wanted a harmonizer. I said, 'Just tell them to put it in the production studio rack. Don't ask about it. Don't worry about it. It's yours.' Even before we were number one, we were also looking out for the Buzzard!"

Maltz would also buy other stations, including the ground-breaking KSAN-FM in San Francisco and one in Los Angeles.

Back in Cleveland, the hippies on one side of the hall and the hillbillies on the other side were generating a lot of opportunities for growth.

The WMMS formula was copied far and wide, and in many cases outright stolen. A jock in Hawaii would take the name Kid Leo, an insurance guy in Phoenix told customers he was known as "Matt the Cat" when he was on radio in Cleveland (not the same guy!), and Murray Saul's Friday "Get Downs" (described in the next chapter) were taped and used on stations around the country.

And in a very competitive Cleveland market, Milt Maltz was

offered a show that would have a huge impact on the local and national radio scene.

"I had a chance to get Howard Stern for WMMS. I turned it down, and I turned it down everywhere at all my stations because he was attacking people who were mentally ill. I heard him say 'People from asylums shouldn't be allowed to walk the streets. They're crazy people.' Come on! They need help. They need psychiatric help. There's medications out there. Life's too short. I don't want that. I'm not going to do that."

By that time Maltz's TV empire was growing as well and in 1992 he left radio to concentrate on television. Two years later, Howard Stern reached the number-one spot and came to Cleveland to hold a massive rally in the Flats to celebrate his victory.

Almost twenty-five years later, Milt Maltz describes the success of the Buzzard this way: "It represented the community of Cleveland, especially the students and the young people. As they grew older they stayed with it, and they cared about it. For some reason there was a sense of 'This is our town and this is our station,' and WMMS worked hard to get there. We didn't use the traditional kind of announcer on the air. We were reality. We were local people who could live next door to you. It was a wonderful experience, and I'm glad I stayed with it. I liked the people that worked here."

He's less enthusiastic about the medium's future.

"There's no future in the radio that I knew. The first mistake was made by President Clinton when he lifted the maximum number of stations you could own. Wall Street people became the media kings. They took over broadcasting. They were only looking at cash flow."

For many people for many years, WMMS was a cornerstone of their lives. Thanks to a deal that fell through in San Diego, we all got to hug the Buzzard.

"Get down, dammit!"

Murray Saul

ONE OF THE STRENGTHS of WMMS was the cast of characters it put on the air. The air staff and music took center stage, but other unique individuals popped in and got people talking.

You could write entire books about Mr. Leonard, who was based in Cleveland for a time and was heard on more than twenty stations. He looked nothing like he sounded, and was just as funny off the air as when he was on the mic. Mr. Leonard could also say things to callers off the air that would never be allowed by the FCC, and who would believe them? "I heard Mr. Leonard drop an F bomb!" Yeah, sure.

There was "Bash," Bill Freeman, a grizzled old jock whose passion for music would sometimes have him arguing with callers who won tickets. "You ever hear of this band?" No. "Then why you going to see them?" The overnight show was called the "BLF Bash," but Bill became Bash to his listeners, who spent many sleepless nights waiting to hear what he would say next. Bash had a subtle sense of humor and loved baseball.

(*A personal note from Mike:* I saw it first hand. Flash Ferenc's dad passed away and I was called to sit in on the Morning Zoo for a few days. At 4 a.m. I heard, "Hey Mike! What are you doing here?" I told Bash what happened and he said, "Sorry to hear that. At least he won't have to see the rest of this Indians season!")

Bash didn't shy away from opinions either. He loved a band called the Texas Tornadoes, and they were featured in a McDonald's spot that aired on his show. One day Bash opened the mic after it aired and said, "You know, BLF fans, it's a damn shame that the best music on the station is on a commercial!" Noted artist

Derek Hess was among his fans, and he can still rattle off Bill's famous sign-off: "Green lights and blue skies to ya! Mama come get your baby boy!"

But no talk about the characters that passed through those halls is complete without Murray Saul.

Murray was a flesh and blood cartoon character. An older guy with hair like Larry Fine of the Three Stooges, Murray had a voice like a fog horn. He was animated when he spoke, so he always drew major attention. At station events, Murray was the face of WMMS, just as the Buzzard was its symbol. Oh, and one more important point: Murray smoked weed. Lots of weed. And he didn't care who knew it.

Murray did a weekly on-air rant every Friday to kick off the weekend, and most of the time it had thinly veiled references to marijuana. Sometimes it was blatant. Some examples:

"It's winter, but I smell the burning of the leaves in the air!

"Twist those tunas and send them around. I talked to an old grizzled prospector this week who struck some gold. It was a little bit of that eighteen-karat gold for sure. Another sign of spring!

"Have our rides pointed in the right direction, have our pockets stuffed with baggies, stuffed with goodies for the road. Spend a little time in the place you like with people you like to go crazy with. Yayza!

"The supply has been kind of lean the last couple of weeks. Everybody is hinting and promising but there's no action. Think about this: If everyone just lit up once and started passing, and passing, and passing . . . Turn on a friend! Get out the bong!

"Fancy looking pipe you got there and it looks nice and clean with a brand new screen! Sure wish we had some twistables to put in there. There's a rumor that a magician is producing gold in baggies nearby. Sure wish we had some of that!

"Let's start stuffing those Thanksgiving tunas with the herbs of the earth! Oh, those sacred herbs! Jamaican sage, Colombian rosemary, Acapulco thyme—and save some to spice up the pumpkin pie!"

One day Gary Dee, in his guise as the Reverend Bornagain, stopped by the production studio during Saul's "get down" taping and piped in, saying, "Oh jeezis! What is this?! Getting our young boys and girls into sin on the weekend at 6 o'clock!" He accused Murray Saul of being a false prophet, smoking the devil's weed and leading Cleveland's youth down a wicked path. The bit ended with Saul and Dee drinking wine and puffing a joint.

Nobody partied like Murray Saul. Just ask Denny Sanders, who had a later shift at WMMS. Sanders says, "Concerts, record company dinners, special events, parties, etc.—I didn't go to as many I as wanted to because I was on the air live every weekday evening, so I could not be the social butterfly that some others at the station were. But I do remember a party hosted by Murray Saul one Saturday night. Murray had an apartment in Cleveland Heights on Euclid Heights Boulevard near Coventry, just a few doors down from the Heights Art Theater. His apartment had a balcony that overlooked the street. Many of us who worked at WMMS lived in the neighborhood in those days, so it was a short walk to Murray's.

"Well, the party was going full blast and Murray himself was pretty blasted. Murray was about twenty years older than we were, but you would never know it! Around 2 a.m., the Heights Art Theater's midnight movie let out. In those pre-cable, pre-home video days, the Saturday night midnight movies at a local theater were all the rage for stoners to watch cartoons, old TV commercials and some crappy B picture for laughs. It was the *Mystery Science Theater 3000* of its day." (They also drew some pretty big crowds, especially when the Heights played *The Rocky Horror Picture Show*.)

"Anyway, the movie lets out and Murray is on his balcony with a wine bottle in one hand and a spliff the size of yule log in the other, making a lot of noise. By this time, Murray was pretty famous, having done the station's TV commercial among other high-visibility appearances. The crowd sees him on the balcony and starts yelling his catchphrase, 'Get down!' Murray, now gloriously blotto,

WHMS: "PRIDE OF CLEVELAND" LP PARTY
January, 1981

Murray Saul's rants put him in the company of rock and roll elite. Here he is enjoying backstage amenities with "Kid Leo" Travagliante.

tells the crowd that he's having a party and to come on up! The next thing we knew, we heard what sounded like a cattle stampede with dozens of people running up the stairs to his second-floor apartment. I said to Murray, 'What the hell are you doing? You don't know who these people are!' He replied 'Don't worry, everyone's my friend!'" Sanders said goodbye and headed out the door.

The next morning, Sanders headed out for a newspaper and passed Saul's place. "There was Murray, sitting on his porch in a blanket like an old Indian. 'Come on up,' he says. I asked him what happened last night, and he replied 'I don't know. I passed out, and when I woke up everybody was gone. They took my stereo speakers, a lamp, some records, and a bunch of other stuff. But you know what hurt the most? They opened the refrigerator and stole my Sunday ham!' He was more upset about the ham than anything else!"

WKRP in . . . Willoughby

Hollywood Lands in Lake County

NO ONE LAUGHED HARDER at TV's *WKRP in Cincinnati* than radio people. Much of it was based on stuff seen first-hand by the show's creator Hugh Wilson, who had worked at WQXI in Atlanta, and on stories passed on as legend through the industry. (That one story line where they threw turkeys out of a helicopter really happened.) But Wilson and his crew did plenty of research, too. After all, writing a weekly show with a main story and a subplot is like feeding a hungry monster. Before the show's pilot episode was filmed, Wilson hit the road to check out the stations and personalities in the top markets, and that included Cleveland.

There was an awful lot of licensed music in the episodes of *WKRP in Cincinnati*. No one foresaw a secondary market in home video back in 1978. That's why some series like *Midnight Caller* (also set in a radio station) don't come to DVD because of expensive music rights. *WKRP* was held up for years because of that. You can now get the complete series in a boxed set, but much of the music has been replaced with generic tunes.

If you watch the show closely, you see a wall in the studio with bumper stickers from the stations they visited. WGCL and WMMS are in that group.

The show's characters bear similarities to some folks in Cleveland. WKRP's Andy Travis had the same blow-dried, layered hair style worn by G98's program director Bob Travis, but so did a lot of program directors trying to straddle the corporate/hip fence. Howard Hesseman, who played Dr. Johnny Fever, actually was a disc jockey at the legendary KSAN in San Francisco, and had known 'GCL's Bob Gott when he was a census taker in Haight

Willoughby got a taste of Hollywood when actor Gordon Jump stopped by to play radio at WELW. *Cleveland Press Collection, Cleveland State University Archives*

Ashbury. Like Fever, Gott had a cup with all the names he used at other stations, including "Grave Disaster." A lot of other stations here and across the country could claim there was a link between themselves and some of the show's characters . . . but only one could tell the tale that happened at WELW.

The call letters stood for "Willoughby-Eastlake-Willowick." The station was two house trailers put together, and it shared a driveway with a private residence. It wasn't much to look at, but it's what came out of the transmitter that counted. It was the voice of Lake County, airing local sports, polkas and popular music, and talk shows with politicians from around the region. Car dealers and local sponsors kept it on the air, and the community supported them for supporting the station. Some parts of the listening area were still pretty rural. Those parts of town were called "Willbilly," and folks depended on that radio link for their information.

WELW prided itself on an exceptional news department. The station never paid much, but that didn't stop some top-notch journalists from cutting their teeth there before moving on to bigger markets. They knew the audience and what they needed to hear, and that formed a strong bond with the folks at home. Joe Jastremski spent a good number of years at WELW before moving on to Akron's WAKR, where he was named "Ohio Newscaster of the Year." He's part of the link to WKRP.

Jastremski was on top of anything happening in Lake County. The Church of Jesus Christ of Latter Day Saints has a long and rich history in Kirtland, where its followers built its first temple in 1836. It welcomes thousands of people of the Mormon faith every year, and now and then you spot a pretty big name in the crowd. Steve Young, the quarterback for the San Francisco 49ers, made the trip, and so did Andrea Kramer, who was a reporter for NBC's *Sunday Night Football*. And one year, that face in the crowd was Gordon Jump, who played Arthur Carlson, *WKRP*'s station manager.

Jump was originally from Dayton, and went to college at Otterbein in Westerville, and he loved coming back to Ohio. He went to grad school at Kansas State for TV and journalism, and was bitten by the radio bug at the college station. After they handed him a diploma in 1957, he started picking up radio and TV jobs, and life was good. He was a born performer, doing kids shows and TV weather, but there was one problem: He was far from a major market, and you didn't make a lot of money in Topeka.

In the early 1960s, Jump converted to the Mormon faith and headed west to try his hand at acting. He got plenty of work, too, but mostly minor roles. You'd see him in bit parts in *Get Smart*, *Green Acres*, *Mary Tyler Moore*, until he hit the big time on *WKRP in Cincinnati*. He kept getting roles after *WKRP*, too, which is kind of odd. When someone defines an iconic role, they often end up typecast and can't find work. Jastremski heard that Jump was in town, and invited him out to WELW, not expecting that he would show.

But he did! Gordon Jump walked through the door at WELW, and he was back in radio. You could hear that he was having a great time, too. He never lost his radio chops, and must have made quite an impression. Jastremski remembers him being there for about an hour, but some listeners claimed he was there for some time beyond that. Legend or not, it was clear that Jump enjoyed being a radio guy again. And, if only for a short time, he turned WELW into WKRP—in Willoughby.

"I didn't saddle up to come in second!"

Gary Dee and People Power

HE WAS THE "FRESNO FLASH," a loud-mouthed, highly opinionated braggart who came in to Cleveland with one goal in mind: to be "Number One in the World." And Gary Dee reached the summit at two Cleveland stations, WERE-AM and WHK-AM. There are hundreds, maybe thousands, of stories about Dee on and off the air. Most of them are true.

By 1972, WERE was a shadow of itself. The station that broke Elvis Presley, Johnny Ray, and so many others in the 1950s had drifted to middle-of-the-road music, and radio superstar Bill Randle had been reduced to doing a "swap and shop" show with listeners trading used items. Randle was their big gun, but the station wasn't about to fight the Top 40 stations with a weak signal and aging air staff. Most of the air staff drifted to other stations. Randle hung on, and you could tell he wasn't happy. Neither was the owner and general manager, Paul Neuhoff. The format didn't generate ratings, and that meant sales were circling the drain. What to do?

Neuhoff knew about Dee's wild radio reputation, or as Dee put it, "frugging in the fig fields in Fresno." Dee was generating numbers and talks were soon underway to bring him to Cleveland to anchor a controversial talk format called "People Power." He would be the morning drive man and the cornerstone of the new format. Randle wasn't having it.

His friends will tell you that Bill Randle had an ego the size of the Terminal Tower and he could back up every word of it. He was a close adviser to Elvis Presley, and turned down a chance to manage him because he was too busy with radio. That opened the door for Colonel Tom Parker to move in, and Randle often regretted that turn of events. Randle also hosted Presley's first show as a rock and roller north of the Mason-Dixon line, third on a Saturday afternoon, Brooklyn High School bill headlined by Pat Boone and Bill Haley & the Comets. Here's a bit of trivia: Presley also performed in a "Hillbilly Hayride" country show sponsored by WERE the night before at the Circle Theater at East 105th and Euclid Avenue. It was hosted by the station's Tommy Edwards, and after Presley opened for Faron Young he sat at a card table in the lobby to greet fans—who pretty much ignored him.

Still, Elvis killed at Brooklyn High, and the performance was filmed as part of a Warner Brothers short about Randle titled *The Pied Piper of Cleveland*. A rough cut of the film was shown once. Randle didn't like it and wouldn't approve distribution until it was re-edited. Carl Reese was at WERE at the time, and he said Randle didn't want to pay for the edit job. No one knows where that film ended up, but there is a standing offer of a million dollars from various collectors with deep pockets hoping to find a print.

Randle could make an artist singlehandedly. The Everly Brothers signed their first recording contract and were told to get on a Greyhound and head to Cleveland to give Randle their first single. Randle got all the new releases first. When he found out that jocks at other stations, like Bud Wendell at WELW, were recording the songs off the air and putting them on their stations, Randle started breaking into the instrumental breaks to announce, "another WERE exclusive on the Bill Randle show." That ended the bootlegs. It was a move that WMMS adapted in later years.

But those days were behind him, and Randle wanted nothing to do with "People Power." When he was told about the new format, he stormed out of the station. But he left something behind. Randle took good care of himself and would often jog around the city before his show. Before the format change, he had demanded the management install a shower for him in the second-floor men's room. He quit the day after it was installed, and the new installation was called "the Bill Randle Memorial Shower" from that point on.

Now it was up to the new guy to give the sales people something to sell.

No one was ready for Gary Dee, and that includes inside the station as well as the audience. There was even a newspaper campaign to have him removed from the air, but that just turned into free publicity. And sometimes Dee would get the other air personalities involved in some very weird programming. John Webster remembers them well.

Webster says Dee went on the air one morning proclaiming, "We live in a world full of liars, and I, Gary Dee, number one in the world, will today lead you in a search for truth. I have in my hand this month's copy of *Psychology Today*, which contains an article which says you cannot lie if you're naked." You know what's coming next. "There goes my shirt." Webster says you could clearly hear his clothes rustling in the background. "Now, my pants, socks and shoes. Hot mercy, Martha! It's cold in here. Can you turn off the air conditioner?" Gary was a master of raising the curtain on the "theater of the mind," and he knew his so-called "Dee-sciples" could envision him stripping down and feeling the chill.

People started calling in and saying they were doing the same, claiming they wanted to try this new approach to finding "truth and justice." Some listeners called to apologize because they were in a public place, and many said they were nude and found themselves unable to lie.

Webster remembers it was a hilarious morning. "There were no complaints, except from an older lady, who told Gary, 'I don't dare disrobe. The sight of me naked would scare my grandkids!'"

A couple of hours later, mild-mannered announcer Howie Lund came in to do his one-hour noon show called "Station Break." It featured a wide variety of guests, and not always the kind found on an average talk show. They could be folks passing through the Greyhound or Trailways bus stations across the street, homeless people, and even "women of ill repute." (Lund never used the word prostitute.) Or they might be politicians or other newsmakers. On this particular day, he, himself, would make news.

After Dee's nude broadcast, Lund asked for candidates to help him further test the theory that naked folks were more honest. Surprisingly, nearly a dozen people packed into the studio, including several attractive young women. A few were WERE employees. Howie closed the studio doors and immediately stripped down. Everybody in the studio followed suit.

Webster remembers the discussion as "interesting, serious, but mostly educational and sometimes downright boring. The nude guests agreed it was tough to tell a lie. There was nothing obscene nor objectionable."

The hour was nearly over when the aggressive *Cleveland Press* columnist Bill Barrett and a photographer shoved their way into the air studio. Howie had his bare feet on the table with the *Psychology Today* magazine in his lap. He was surrounded by a dozen nude people, sitting cross-legged on the floor. A WEWS-TV cameraman had come to the station to do a story on a volunteer group, Call for Action, that operated out of the WERE basement. He heard what was happening and rushed upstairs to the studio.

The camera just caught guests putting on their clothes. The story led the six o'clock news, but the footage was far from sensational.

The *Cleveland Press* played it differently. Shortly after 3 p.m., when the first edition hit the streets, the front-page headline was "NAKED RADIO ON WERE!" There were pictures of Howie, sitting with the magazine in his lap, surrounded by other naked guests. Barrett's narrative was scathing, and he promised to file a complaint with the FCC. Luckily for WERE, he didn't—but he still put a scare into the station's management. They immediately sent telegrams to the commission, offering tape recordings and pleading—get this—the "educational nature" of the broadcast. The FCC bought WERE's story. There were no citations, not even a warning.

The next rating period, WERE had climbed to the number

one spot in Cleveland. The station sent Barrett a big bouquet of flowers, the latest rating book, and a hammer. The thank you card invited the columnist to "Come bash us anytime."

Gary Dee continued making headlines with his wild morning talk show, calling older women callers "barracudas," and targeting media figures and politicians with an Arkansas accent that he played up on the air. He worked with a bunch of very creative guys, including his producer Bob Gott, who he'd met in Fresno, and Peter Chin, who worked the phones when he wasn't helping produce the show. His family owned a very popular Chinese restaurant in Cleveland, but Chin was in his element in radio. He also took calls during Cleveland City Council President George Forbes' show which ran right after Dee's, and found he could do a dead-on impression of Forbes. One day, Forbes was late for his show and Chin just put on the headphones, clicked on the mic, and did his impression. No one was the wiser, including the news staff, who didn't know Forbes was late until they saw him walking through the newsroom, laughing on his way to the air studio. He'd been listening in his car.

Dee's most infamous show happened on December 11, 1974. Cleveland was a different then. It had a tired, beat up downtown that few people saw reason to visit after the work day. The nightlife that once lit up the theater district and Public Square had faded away. Even the legendary Roxy Burlesque had phased out strippers in favor of soft porn films. A hole-in-the-wall, make-shift theater on Prospect called the New Era brought in bottom-feeder entertainers who were on the road when they weren't in front of a camera. That's where Dee and his crew found Honeysuckle Divine.

To say her act was truly disgusting would have been a compliment. Much of the stage show was Divine lying on her back and shooting objects at drunken patrons from her "orifice." Use your own imagination, and then go to confession. Yeah, that's how bad it was. She also wrote a column for *Screw* magazine, and publisher Al Goldstein once claimed he'd hired an armed guard to keep her

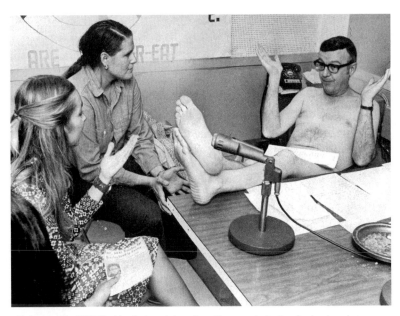

Naked truth. WERE's Howie Lund drew headlines and plenty of raised eyebrows when he did his entire show in the nude. *Cleveland Press Collection, Cleveland State University Archives*

away from him. Honeysuckle Divine was now going to do morning drive radio in a major market!

The show started with a commercial for Mr. Jingeling at Halle's department store, inviting kids to come down and share the holiday spirit. The People Power jingles ended the news segment with John Webster's voice over thundering horns proclaiming WERE "your newspaper of the airwaves!" Fortunately, there was a local newspaper strike at the time, and TV wasn't about to cover this. Next up was sportscaster Bob Neal, a very sophisticated broadcaster who sensed this was not a show he wanted to be a part of.

Dee introduced himself as "Gary Dee, D.D.—Doctor of Divinity," who intended to save Honeysuckle Divine and her companion, a sword swallower named Count Desmond. Neal said his money was on Dee to "withstand the temptations of Satan." The FCC might be a different battle.

John Webster recalls, "The morning of the broadcast, the program director decided to listen at home, because he felt the studio staff had been sufficiently warned. It was a very bad decision!"

That would become evident when Divine joined the show at 7:30, the crucial point of morning drive. Dee stated that he was providing her access to radio waves that belonged to the public under "the Herbert Hoover Amendment of 1934." That same public might not have approved if it had a say beforehand. Even Dee suggested before the interview that he would soon be "in a whole mess of trouble!" Neal gave a disclaimer, asked that the show not be linked in any way to him or his family and urged parental discretion. Enter Honeysuckle Divine.

Dee played another disclaimer from station voice Brian Hodgkinson advising, "Some of the events heard on WERE are produced solely for information." Dee himself took on many roles in that show. He became a raging evangelist, a porn fighter, a carnival barker, and he even offered to manage Divine. She described in detail what her act was all about, said she was amazed at the number of couples who came to her show, and claimed her act actually turned people off to sex. It was people turning off their radios that should have been the major concern.

Webster recalls Dee expressed outrage at her "sinful ways," but promised her "salvation, if you'll repent." And then the words that made management shudder. "But *before* you repent, could you play us a tune?" Divine produced a horn and said she would play "Jingle Bells." The horn never got near her mouth.

Here's the way Webster remembers it:

"The program director grabbed the phone and dialed the studio hotline, but it was busy. He dialed repeatedly, and finally the line rang over and over before engineer Tony Pollock answered. He said 'Hey, boss I'm having trouble hearing because the whole damn sales department is packed into the control room, egging on Gary.'

"The program director yelled 'Cut it, Tony,' but Pollock yelled back 'What did you say? It's too noisy in here.' It was too late. The one-minute tape delay had played out. The flute continued." But would the station?

Divine stayed with Dee until the end of the show and the damage was done. Almost immediately there were calls for the program director's head. Many of the department heads who were now saying the programming was out of control had been drooling in the control room just a few minutes before. General manager Paul Neuhoff called the whole morning crew into his office, and it wasn't to congratulate them. After a tense exchange and a few threats, the morning show promised to be more careful and everyone walked out of the office rubbing their backsides but still employed.

There was a lot of controversy on that station, so WERE recorded every show on a "logger tape," a reel-to-reel recording at 1⅞ speed, just in case. That's slow enough to record twelve hours of programming on each side of the reel. The reel mysteriously disappeared just after the Honeysuckle Divine show, and oddly enough showed up stuffed in back of a tape console in the production studio five years later.

The CBS radio network had been with WERE since it first went on the air, and outraged listeners began calling New York to complain. Back in Cleveland, Bob Gott insisted there was no tape of the show but CBS didn't buy it. The network got so many complaints that it dropped the station as an affiliate, and wouldn't be back for years to come.

Dee stayed on until WERE, bleeding red ink despite huge ratings that it couldn't sell, changed to an all-news format. Dee went down the street to WHK.

Dee had a very colorful life. He was married for a time to Liz Richards, a TV host at WEWS. Their battles off the air got plenty of newspaper coverage, and Dee used it as the basis for some of his most memorable shows. He made headlines on his own, as well, like when he staged a sit-in protest shutting down a bridge that was scheduled to be razed. The protest did successfully block traffic and call attention to the bridge. Unfortunately, Dee shut down the

Gary Dee (left) at the Gray Bar Motel. Dee and Cuyahoga County Sheriff Gerald McFaul were old friends, but that didn't stop the law from putting Dee in the slammer. *Cleveland Public Library*

wrong bridge. The one he wanted was a few blocks away.

But competition from FM, especially WHK's sister station WMMS, was making Dee's job tougher every day. WMMS program director John Gorman says he saw that transition because it was taking Dee longer to get out of character after his show. Plus, he enjoyed a cocktail.

You never knew how sober or in what mood Gary Dee was when he walked in the door. Jim Endsley found that out the hard way. That was only one of the names he used at various stations. He was also known as Fred Wesley, Fred Winthrop, and Jim Lovejoy, and he would take just about any shift because he enjoyed working in the business. Endsley was working overnight at WHK and would hand it off to Gary Dee when he took over for morning drive. Dee stumbled in one morning after a rough night, and Endsley smelled trouble. WHK reduced its power overnight, and it was the job of the operator on duty to increase it. The computers were really primitive—green dot matrix letters on a black screen with no pictures and a bunch of numbers and symbols. There were bubbles popping in front of Dee's face, but it was time to go and guess who had to increase the power?

"Gary, we have to do this in the proper sequence. Let me show you—"

"Shut up!" he snapped. "I'm a radio professional! You don't tell me what to do or how to do it!"

Endsley's heart was pounding. "Gary, it's important that—"

"Get out!"

Endsley went to the restroom just outside the studio to wash his hands and heard the signal deteriorate on the overhead speaker as the station went off the air. He ran back into the studio.

"Gary I tried to tell you—"

"Why you rotten bastard! How dare you! You didn't tell me anything! You're trying to get me fired." That was the last thing Endsley heard before Dee swung around and clocked him square in the head. Endsley crumbled onto the floor, out cold.

Endsley didn't know how long he was out. He just remembers coming to and seeing Gary doing his show. Endsley quietly crawled out of the studio on his hands and knees, made it to his car, and sat there trying to get his head together. He might have been unconscious for most of an hour. That's when it hit him: Whoever reset the computer to get Dee back on the air had to step over him to get to the computer. They had just let him lie there!

Dee would also tempt fate and have Honeysuckle Divine back on the air when he set up shop at WHK. He never shied away from controversy one bit. At one point, he suggested that the Muscular Dystrophy telethon was keeping Jerry Lewis's career alive, and when Lewis heard about it, he came back at Dee like a lion! Dee ended up delivering a face-to-face apology to Lewis on the air.

When FM became the "go to" format, though, Dee saw the writing on the wall and looked to other markets. WHK's country

Amen and alleluia! Gary Dee could easily switch his on-air personality to any number of characters depending on the guest and topic.

format reverted back to a rock and roll oldies format called "14K," and for a time Cleveland was without the man known as "the Mouth of the Cuyahoga."

When Dee returned to Cleveland after failed attempts in New York and Washington, D.C., he got the midday gig at WWWE. He was still funny, but he often went to extremes. The show would dip to new lows, but Dee could bounce back. He could keep you glued to the radio until the payoff, and knew how to bring it home.

During one of Cleveland's hottest summers in the late 1980s, Dee came on the air screaming, "I'll get you for this! You can't do this to me! You can't do this to Cleveland! You won't get away with this!" Listeners were sitting in their cars in 90-degree heat, late for work but waiting to hear what Dee was screaming about and who he was threatening. Finally, breathless and in a strained, raspy voice, Dee gasped out, "Global warming! The ozone layer! It's gone, and they did it! [TV news people] Wilma Smith and Mark Koontz! All their hair spray!"

Fired for Being Herself

Shauna Zurbrugg, Fighting for
Rights in a Kangaroo Court

THE EARLIEST DAYS OF the Cleveland FM rock scene were full of young people with high ideals. They were going to change the world for the better, and FM rock would be their podium. They didn't get paid a lot because for most it was their first gig, but no one seemed to care. They were there to promote the hippie ideals. Shauna Zurbrugg was among them, but her experience here was far less than ideal.

Shauna would go on to a successful career in radio and production on the West Coast, even winning a Grammy for her work on Hillary Clinton's audio book. But her days in Ohio had a profound influence.

"As with so many of us, music inspired my world in the Sixties and early Seventies," Shauna recalls. "One of the stations I was drawn to was WNCR. Very few people were listening to FM radio in those days, but it was 'underground' and also in stereo—something AM radio could not provide. I listened to the music with awe, and loved hearing the DJs explain the background of a record, such as who wrote it, who was on drums, bass, etc. I was entertained and informed. The intimate feeling delivered by WNCR DJs brought one closer to the speakers and into a cocoon of seeming familiarity with whoever was on the air, making our lives richer with the music they chose."

Those were the days when there were long musical breaks and you could call the jock and talk about anything on your mind. Shauna took that opportunity.

"Late at night in the fall of 1970, I was alone in the house and felt compelled to call WNCR to speak to DJ David Spero. He had told his listeners he was available for one-on-one chats off-air if anyone was interested. At the time I was in college but living at home, and I was bored. I wanted to connect with someone who shared my interest in music, and David seemed to be a very approachable person. So I dialed the number and—voila!—David answered."

It was a phone call that would change her life.

"I was not, in my mind, a 'fan' calling. I was simply a friend who loved having another special friend who was also in entertainment. I was captivated with the new culture, and inspired by the diversity and urgency in the music."

The two had an immediate connection.

"Over the next few months, I would call to say hello about once a week, sometimes for an hour at a time." While those calls gave her inspiration, it was a radio spot that gave her direction.

"While driving home from class one evening, listening to WNCR, I heard an ad for the Specs Howard School of Broadcast Arts. It was truly one of those 'a-ha!' moments. In a second, I realized how becoming a DJ could be an easy way to make a name for myself in entertainment without doing the summer stock route of acting in theater after theater. It was also at the peak of women's liberation and I gleaned that very few women were on radio—AM or FM—and that my love of music, entertaining and genuine ambition could be parlayed into a different medium that I would enjoy while aiding my acting goals. It was clear to me that the timing was perfect, as everyone in most industries were feeling the social pressure to hire women in positions normally known as platforms for men only."

Shauna had a plan, but now she had to deal with her parents. It turned out to be easier than she thought.

"At home that evening" she recalls, "I proposed to my parents that I drop out of college, go up to Cleveland, and take a course in broadcasting at Specs Howard. They agreed! Both parents always supported my showbiz desires; thus, no conflicts occurred with my decision."

WNCR's David Spero was happy to give out advice and opinions on and off the air. For aspiring jocks, he was just a phone call away. *Courtesy of David Spero*

Shauna loved the feel of the school and radio in general.

"I learned how to use a mic, turntable, run tapes, edit tapes, etc. Plus, local radio personnel came to the class to lend additional info. One of the guest speakers was WNCR's Lee Andrews, a very pleasant and professional DJ I often listened to and admired."

That also led to visits to the WNCR air studio while jocks were doing their shows. Those visits would prove to be very important for a kid hoping to get on the air.

"Most of the time, I would drop by after my class before driving a one-hour schelp to my home in Alliance, south of Cleveland. It was at WNCR that I finally met David Spero, where we hugged and chatted like old friends. I grew to know David and Lee as the months went on due to several snow storms where no one could drive in the city or anywhere else. We were often stranded. WNCR's station was situated in the Statler Hilton Hotel, where

WNCR had several rooms always on reserve for guests and staff. Many a night—without "escapades" of any sort—were spent in those rooms, chatting the night away with Lee, David and others. I often had a few friends with me who would enliven the scene."

Not the traditional way of getting a job, but it proved effective. Shauna arranged for a weekday look-around at WNCR's administrative offices, and was introduced to another key player.

"I was a few months away from graduating from Specs, and although I didn't plan to be hired at WNCR as no openings were available, particularly for a beginner, I did want to gain the overall feel of the basic workings of a radio station, from the news department to management. While waiting in the lobby for the elevator to go up to the WNCR offices, I glanced at a man who had sidled up beside me, also waiting. He was wearing the most amazing jacket I'd ever seen! It was adorned with several sewn-on logos of bands and music icons, with suede-frays hanging from the sleeves. It was the epitome of hip! The man was also wearing a leather beret and wreaked of style and intense energy. When we stepped into the elevator we realized we were both going up to the WNCR studios and began a simple chat. He said his name was Billy Bass, a DJ at the AM hit station, WIXY. I had heard of Billy, but did not listen to AM radio. All I knew was that a sexy, hip, and cool guy in radio was sharing an elevator with me and that he had made an impression I would never forget."

As it turns out, Billy was there for an important reason.

Even though WIXY was by far the top station in town, longer and more reflective music was being introduced, and FM radio embraced it. Plus, the FM jocks had a lot more freedom on the air. Billy had decided to head back to the FM dial where he had started, at WMMS in 1968. He was hired as WNCR's program director, and his plate was full right from the start.

"Billy was on the air at WNCR in the Prime evening time slot, making his way through the new company and changing the programming into a plethora of expansive music programming," Shauna says. "He made very few on-air talent changes, choosing

Shauna Zurbrugg saw a constant learning curve in
radio, and some of those lessons were pretty tough—
especially on women. *Courtesy of Shauna Zurbrugg*

instead to work with most of the existing jocks and those in the
news department. He brought fresh ideas to everything—and it
was working. The ratings began to climb, and as with David and
Lee, I found myself hanging out in-studio with Billy a few times a
week while he did his shows as I traveled between my radio class
and the station."

It was also a true learning experience, especially in developing
the FM rock style.

"Through Billy, and later Martin Perlich, I learned how to create a seamless segue, how to properly hold the record and meld it into the next tune without a jarring transition. I was mesmerized by Billy's on-air personality and voice. I also liked him in general, and had fun laughing with him and his many cronies who would drop by to hang out."

But Billy was still management, and that sometimes means making tough choices. According to Shauna, he didn't really care for the morning drive team.

"He thought they were bland and boring. The wife was the only woman on FM radio in the region at the time, and he felt a stronger female personality would be better for the station in general. He turned to me and said, 'You're in broadcasting school, right? Well, why don't you make a tape for me and let's see where it goes.'"

Shauna rushed to the Specs Howard studio to get her audition tape together. A week later, life changed dramatically. She says in a classic show-biz-type moment, she gave the tape to Billy who gave it a listen and, "to my glee and shock, literally picked me up and swung me around saying, 'You're the girl I've been looking for all of my life!'"

But there was a catch. Billy still wanted a male/female morning show, and Shauna could have the gig if she could find a guy to share the mic. She didn't have to look far.

"Fortunately, I had a friend at Kent State who did a radio show for the campus station. I convinced him to make a tape with me and, if hired, to leave Kent and go directly into broadcasting, which had not been his goal. He was a business major. Although he looked a lot like Frank Zappa in those days, he was very conservative with his future plans. It wasn't an easy sell, but he eventually agreed to make a tape and to have me present it to Billy. My friend was Jeff Gelb."

Within a month Jeff and Shauna were on the air. It was a busy time for Jeff, leaving college, finding a home, and putting together a show with Shauna that people would listen to. It came together pretty quickly, with Jeff and Shauna learning the arts of interview-

Decades before eBay, Shauna and her radio partner Jeff Gelb were connecting their audience members who had products to sell or trade on "People's Want Ads." *Courtesy of Jeff Gelb*

ing, back and forth banter, hosting concerts, and even "People's Want Ads," with listeners trading goods and services on the air. (They even gave out the listeners' home phone numbers!) But this was radio, where things change rapidly. They sure did for Jeff and Shauna.

Less than a year after Jeff and Shauna debuted, Billy was offered the program director's gig at WMMS. Nationwide Communications, part of the insurance giant, owned WNCR and that meant corporate influence. 'MMS offered a lot more freedom, and Billy took David Spero and Martin Perlich with him. Shauna was angry.

"Billy and I were friends! I was confused and hurt that he hadn't

Billy Bass's defection from WNCR to WMMS shook up the Cleveland radio scene. Shauna Zurbrugg would have rather jumped ship, too, than stay at WNCR.

asked me to join him in the new venture. I decided not to speak to him again.

"During the transition, a PD from an AM Top 40 station in Detroit was brought to WNCR as Billy's replacement. I was given my own show, as was Jeff, who continued in the morning slot with the 'Want Ads.' Joyce Halasa, who had been doing promotions at WMMS, was placed on the air by Billy against my time slot. Joyce and I were friends and never had a competitive element in place. However, despite now having my own show, I was seething inside that my mentor and 'friend' Billy chose a non-DJ as the only woman on his station. I didn't understand his motives."

Those would be the least of Shauna's problems.

The new guy at 'NCR targeted some folks on the air, and Shauna was on the list.

"Many of us played music based on our moods, which had

always been a successful element in most of the DJs' programming at that time," Shauna recalls. "As most of us were 'hippies' and not accustomed to following corporate directives, we found our show's inspiration through new music we had just discovered, combined with what was happening in our lives. We were not accustomed to being micromanaged in any way other than following FCC rules.

"When I returned from a holiday vacation wherein I had a sad discovery of a love that had gone wrong, I recall playing 'I'm A Loser' by the Beatles while the PD stood sternly behind a glass window aimed into our studio glaring at what he would later deem to be my 'unprofessionalism.' Never mind that my ratings were great. The daily intimidation definitely curbed my inspiration and programming freedom. I'm sure a strained sound emanated from my throat as I did my back and front announcements.

"Meanwhile, I began receiving calls at home from Joyce telling me that she didn't want to be on the air and asking would I go over to WMMS and take her slot? I insisted I would never do so unless Billy asked me—himself, not via a surrogate. This routine went on for several weeks, perhaps a month or more."

While all of this was happening, an unfortunate incident went down that Shauna now admits was unprofessional on her part.

"I can only justify my actions as a combination of desperation and naivete," she says. "Note I was only nineteen at the time. It was early 1972, and during the Seventies and later the Eighties, sexual experimentation with bisexuality was typical in most music, artistic, and collegiate circles. I was experimenting, and, in the early Seventies, almost anywhere beyond L.A. and New York, finding others who shared a similar interest was not easy. I was not one to seek gay bars. I lived my life having experiences as they happened, organically. But I was lonely. And lost.'"

Then, just as she, herself, had done years before, a listener called in just to talk. It was a call she would regret answering.

Shauna remembers it to this day.

"One day, off-air, I received a call during my show from a young girl claiming to be gay and not knowing where to go to meet other women. I had no concrete advice, but did suggest a few areas she could check out. She continued to question me about my own sexuality, and I admitted that I had an interest and knew other women of the same ilk . . . but couldn't really help. I asked that she call back in a few days and by then I might have more info for her.

"When a week went by without hearing from her, my own desire to meet other women who had a similar proclivity began to escalate. I decided that maybe I should meet her. During the reading of the 'People's Want-Ads' I asked for that listener to call into the station as I had new info for her. I did this for approximately three days, twice a day. I kept it non-personal, but, it was clearly to certain ears a personal request."

Okay, so there was no contact, but storm clouds were brewing.

"I dropped it and carried on. A few weeks later, I found myself suddenly on the verge of being fired based on 'budget reasons' per the general manager. Because my ratings were good and I always showed-up for my gig, I was confused. Why me? Other DJs were also confused. Jeff, Doyle and a few others, went to the GM and offered to split their salaries with me just to keep me on board. They were passionate supporters, and several were ready to quit in protest. Management became a bit concerned that they might lose over half their air-staff."

It looked like a mutiny. Laid back hippies or not, the jocks stood their ground and, more importantly, stood with Shauna. What happened next would never fly today.

"The ruckus that ensued caused our GM to call a meeting where a vote would be taken between management and talent regarding whether or not I should remain at the station. To this day I don't know why I bothered to show up. But I did.

"The news team, administration, and on-air talent were gathered in the conference room around a very long, and quite full, table. Management had decided that the news department would be part of management, and whatever they voted would be for that side. Naturally, job security and so on held sway in many minds on that side of the table despite pleasant personal relationships.

During the well-over-an-hour debate, I listened as cohorts dissected my skills, personality, etc. I watched supporters literally pound the conference table on my behalf as being an incredible on-air personality and a plus to the station's credibility. I also saw people cry on my behalf, and guilt in the eyes of those on the news team for supporting management. When things became extremely acrimonious, I left the room, sat down on the floor outside of the room in the hallway, and simply held my head in dour resignation. When Jeff and Doyle came out to check on me, I pleaded with them to stop fighting. I said, 'If I am not wanted here for some reason, I don't want to be here anymore. Please stop. Keep your jobs. Thank you, but I am over this and I will go.'"

And go she did. But there's more to the story.

"A year later I was told by a former coworker and DJ at WMMS, that the girl who had called me was the daughter of our GM and had set me up in a sting to prove that I was gay and not worthy of my job. My announcements for the girl to contact me did not help. However, the bottom line was discrimination—something I was too young to realize at the time and too traumatized to accept as the reason for being fired. Jeff, Doyle, Lee and others had no idea that this was the primary reason for my demise at WNCR."

So what about WMMS? Shauna ended up there a short time later, but she still wanted to act. She left for L.A. in 1972 and got a gig at KMET, run by former WMMS general manager David Moorehead. Other opportunities arose, and Shauna went on to a long career in a number of high-profile jobs in the southern California entertainment scene. Billy Bass, Jeff Gelb, and Martin Perlich ended up there as well, to reminisce about the old days in Cleveland—some of them good, some of them bad.

Meeting the Beatles

AFTER THE PAYOLA SCANDALS of the 1950s, rock and roll and the stations that played it were on life support. The IRS nailed Alan Freed in New York and Joe Finan in Cleveland, Chuck Berry went to jail, Jerry Lee Lewis pretty much ended his rock and roll career when he married an underaged cousin, Little Richard went to the ministry, and Elvis Presley was in the Army. There were some Motown acts, and the Beach Boys were starting to get some attention, but overall radio was pretty bland.

Novelty records were hot, but they had a short shelf life. One of the hot records of the early Sixties was a song by the old codger who played Grandpappy Amos McCoy on TV's *The Real McCoys*, Walter Brennan, singing about a dead mule named "Old Rivers." In January 1964, you had "Wives and Lovers," a cocktail lounge song by Jack Jones that may be the most sexist tune ever played on the radio. It talks about how tough the old man had it, and wives should be lovers and "run to his arms when he came home to you." Wow.

Everything changed for rock and roll stations the night of February 9, 1964, when Ed Sullivan said, "Ladies and gentlemen, the Beatles!"

Everybody wanted a piece of the Beatles, and the number of jocks around the country claiming to be "the fifth Beatle" could fill Public Hall.

Thousands of fans showed up just to get a glimpse of the Beatles getting off planes or looking out a hotel window, and lots of folks went to extreme measures to even get closer to them. Chances were, though, that the only way to get anywhere near them was to buy a ticket. Don't believe the stories that they waved at people from tour buses. That never, ever happened. The Beatles would fly

WHK sponsored the first Beatles show in Cleveland in 1964. The air staff had access before the show and spent some quality time with the Fab Four. *George Shuba*

in, get in a limo, maybe have a press conference, do the show and spend the rest of the time at the hotel before they moved on to the next city. There was one so-called radio personality with a brokered show who claimed that because his daughter loved Ringo, he hid him in their basement and surprised her. Is there a picture, maybe? Didn't think so. Even so, some radio folks—very few—did have contact with the Beatles and had stories to tell.

When the Beatles played Cleveland in 1964 and 1966, the jocks at WHK and WIXY had some limited access because each station hosted a show. But that was at the press availability event or the concert. A few, like Jerry G. Bishop at KYW, got access at a couple of other shows on the tour because the station had 50,000 watts and could be heard in Florida. It was another guy at KYW, the news anchor Art Schreiber, who really hit pay dirt.

It was late summer 1964, and the Beatles were causing mayhem in every city they played. Schreiber was an old-style news guy, the kind with a press pass in his fedora and cigarette smoke swirling around him as he banged on a typewriter. He had a voice that was so deep that it started in the basement. Schreiber also knew a good story, and when the opportunity arose he wanted to follow the Beatles on their 1964 tour. He would be granted full access, and even fly on the band's private plane.

There was a little snag, though. The KYW news director, who was no fan of the Beatles or Schreiber, wanted no part of it. The 1964 presidential election was coming up, and the candidates were spending plenty of time shaking hands and kissing babies. Schreiber was told to stay home—until a higher power had his say. The general manager knew that the Fab Four, not Lyndon Johnson or Barry Goldwater, would bringing in the listeners, and word came down that Schreiber would be going on the Beatles tour. This reversal endeared Schreiber even less to the news director. He was pretty sure this would be his last high-profile gig before his boss found a way to fire him.

Schreiber joined the tour and was introduced to the world of Beatlemania. Screaming crowds in city after city, back on the plane to the next town, and all he had to do was keep up, do interviews, and feed them back to the station over the phone. Plus, it was fun on the plane! There were only so many seats, and the Beatles turned out to be very affable. They would go from seat to seat and carry on long conversations, and it wasn't long before everyone was on a first-name basis. Schreiber played Monopoly and cards with the guys and joked and listened to their stories. There was only one rule: no autographs. Didn't matter to Schreiber—yet.

The news director back at KYW would bite his lip whenever he heard the reports. He hated to be overruled by upper management, and couldn't stand the Beatles even though his teenage daughter was nuts for the band. The trouble started when she found out one of her dad's employees was on the tour. She saw the band in Cleveland, and at one point even waved at Paul McCartney, who looked right at her (along with thousands of other screaming girls).

Schreiber then got the call that he didn't want: The boss needs Paul's autograph for his daughter. Gulp!

Let's call this girl Kathy. The North American tour was drawing to a close. Schreiber was pretty sure his boss would look to replace him for any reason, and the autograph—or lack of one—would seal the deal. Too bad, too. He liked KYW. He sat on the plane staring off into space, when who should wander by but Paul himself.

"Art. What's wrong? Why the long face?" Schreiber explained the situation, and stressed he would live by the same rules for the other press guys. No autographs, but it looked like no paychecks in the near future.

McCartney lived by those rules, too, but he gave him a smile and said, "Got an idea." He took Schreiber's tape recorder, and they had a conversation with the two talking about the tour, including Cleveland. McCartney said he noticed one girl waving at him, and described her from information Schreiber had given him. Schreiber gave her name, and McCartney said, "Kathy, you stood out and I wanted to say hi! Thanks for being a fan!"

The tour ended, Schreiber returned home and told his boss, "Sorry. Absolutely no autographs—but here." When the news director's daughter played the tape there was a loud scream before she played it over and over and over for anyone who would listen.

Oh, and Art Schreiber had a job at KYW long after the news director had moved on.

The Buzzard—Behind the Curtain

More Stories from WMMS

WMMS WASN'T JUST AN important radio station. For some time, it was very likely the most important radio station in the country. It broke acts, started trends, and reaped huge ratings and revenue for Malrite Broadcasting. The Buzzard soared high above the rest.

If imitation is the most sincere form of flattery, WMMS was constantly being flattered. Murray Saul's Friday "get downs" were taped by other stations and rebroadcast around the country, though Cleveland references were edited out of the bootleg copies. Jocks' names were copied. Years after the originals had become legends in Cleveland, there was a Matt the Cat in Boston, and a Kid Leo in Hawaii.

The Buzzard logo had its imitators, too. Some did their own versions, and others lifted David Helton's original and attached their call letters. When that happened you saw just how efficient the station's legal team could be.

Sometime you didn't need lawyers. The late Len "The Boom" Goldberg was one of the kindest and most understanding people you ever met. But he also guarded the WMMS brand with an iron fist. Some Clevelanders may recall the plaster Buzzard banks that popped up in the late 1970s. There were two sizes, large and small, with the Buzzard in a superhero outfit smoking a joint against a Cleveland backdrop. You saw them in just about every head shop in Northeast Ohio. The guys marketing the banks thought they could sell a lot more if WMMS helped promote them. Keep in mind that those guys had not asked permission to produce them in the first place. Boom was helping market the station, and their call was directed to him. He heard the pitch and said, "Hey! Great

They called him "Boom" for a reason! Len Goldberg had a voice that started in the basement, and he could shake the walls just by saying "hello."

idea! Bring all of them down to the station, and the molds, too."

A few days later dozens of Buzzard banks were lined up in a room at the Statler Office Tower, the casting molds sat on a desk, and the folks behind them greeted Boom with huge smiles on their faces. He asked if he could have one of each bank, they happily agreed, and Boom took them into another room. He returned with a baseball bat and smashed every one of the remaining banks and the molds as the "bankers" looked on in horror. Then, with a dramatic sweep of his arm, Boom pointed the bat at them and said in no uncertain terms, "Next time it's *you!*" Len could be very persuasive.

Celebrities gravitated toward WMMS. A typical day might see actor Jon Cryer and Aaron Neville chatting in the break room waiting their turn for the morning zoo, with Lou Reed stopping by for a midday chat with Matt the Cat, and, later in the day, Brian May of Queen tuning his guitar in the lobby for a quick shot in afternoon drive. "Southside Johnny" Lyon sang Christmas carols at the staff's holiday party. Artists like Chris Whitley might stop by with a load of pizzas for an impromptu party, strumming songs on his National Steel guitar while everyone dug in.

Sometimes the visits didn't go as planned.

When the movie *Light of Day* was being filmed in Cleveland, Michael J. Fox and Joan Jett spent a lot of time at the station. According to WMMS on-air personality Dia Stein, Jett's presence was evident long after she left the building, fouling the hallway rest room so badly that it was unusable for the rest of the day. Put on the fan, close the door, and don't open it until tomorrow. Strange odors weren't uncommon at the station. The supply closet next to the break room was right next to a vent from the deli twelve floors below. Over the years, the vent sprung some leaks but that wasn't necessarily a bad thing. It's just that every time you got a fresh reel of tape it smelled like corned beef.

It seemed like there was always someone famous in the lobby. Gabe Kaplan from *Welcome Back, Kotter* started his sports talk career at a Malrite station on the West Coast and made a pilgrimage to Cleveland to outline his plans. When former kid star Danny Bonaduce found work at Malrite's station in Philadelphia, he would occasionally get some unwanted publicity and get called to the woodshed on the the 12th floor of the Statler. "Hey! Danny Bonaduce! What brings you to Cleveland?" Nervously, he answered, "Aaagh! Chaffee's going to kick my ass!"

*   *   *

A personal note from Mike: Ed O'Neill went on to play Jake Pritchard on ABC's *Modern Family*, but years before he redefined situation comedies as Al Bundy on *Married . . . with Children*. O'Neill was in town to visit with his longtime friend Tim Hagan, at the time a Cuyahoga County commissioner. The two had stayed close since they were kids in Mahoning County, and while O'Neill was in town, he took the time to plug *Married . . . with Children*, which was on Fox. Malrite's WOIO was the Fox affiliate at the time, so it made sense for him to stop by WMMS.

Ed O'Neill did not look like Al Bundy, which shows his depth as an actor when he became that character. No one knew who he was, and he just sat there. I came out to introduce myself, and we walked back to the news department.

Playboy magazine would send out promotional issues every month, and the latest was sitting on a desk as we walked into the news booth. This was the same small booth that Cliff Baechle used for news on WHK, and there was barely room for two chairs and a console. O'Neill didn't mind. I rolled tape, and we chatted as he flipped through the magazine. Suddenly, the door flew open and Ed "Flash" Ferenc took a look around the booth and grabbed the magazine without saying two words. O'Neill was surprised, but we just picked up the interview from there.

Baechle had a very nice watch that he used to time his newscasts, and he would keep it in that small studio. If the interview went well, I would give the watch to the guest as a parting gift, and I handed it over to O'Neill. When we finished our talk I asked him for a favor. His Al Bundy was one of my heroes, and I brought along a camera. I asked for a photo, and he said, "Sure!" I had one shot left in that camera and asked Flash to take the picture. Of course, he started screwing around and I said, "Please just take the picture!" I hoped he got it. As I led him out to the lobby, O'Neill said, "Hey, thanks again for this watch!" Cliff Baechle darted out of his seat and grabbed it off his wrist. (He'd seen that same watch go out the door before, once making it as far as Wilkes-Barre, Pennsylvania.) As we said goodbye and shook hands, O'Neill smiled and said, "This has been the strangest interview I've ever done!"

A week later, I got the photos back. There was no photo with Ed O'Neill—but there was one of me with Al Bundy! That shot hangs on my wall to this day.

* * *

WMMS moved to the Skylight Office Tower overlooking the Avenue at Tower City. The station had floor-to-ceiling glass and was wide open to anyone in the mall—and we saw plenty. You had a bird's eye view when celebrities like Rod Stewart, Michael Jordan, Hillary Clinton, or any number of notable names would walk the mall. Some would walk early in the day. It wasn't unusual to see Beatles producer George Martin or writer Quentin Crisp among many others checking out storefronts before they opened. But people could also see what was going on inside the station.

In August 1994, sister station WHK was now doing morning talk and was not afraid of high-profile guests with little discretion. Teri Weigel had been *Playboy's* April 1986 "Playmate of the Month" and had gotten quite a bit of TV and film work. When those roles stopped coming, she turned to very graphic adult entertainment, and she came to WHK to promote her Cleveland appearance. Fortunately, the offices had yet to open for business, and there were very few people in the station. Within minutes after arriving she was walking around the station completely nude and posing for lurid photos with the hosts.

That same day, the Rolling Stones were in town as part of their Voodoo Lounge tour. Original bass player Bill Wyman had retired from the group some years before to be replaced by an ace session man, Darryl Jones, who agreed to stop by the WMMS morning show. As he walked to the studio he was passed in the hall by the very nude Teri Weigel. Jones squinted his eyes, shook his head and said, "You guys can play with Mick Jagger. I want to work here!"

Belly Up To The Bar

The River of Booze that Fueled Radio

BARS AND OTHER WATERING holes were a big part of the WMMS lifestyle. They could be dive bars or elegant taverns, but if they advertised on 'MMS, they drew huge crowds. Plus, the jocks could seriously add to their income if they did a weekly appearance. The client would add a talent fee, usually a hundred bucks an hour, and was almost assured of extra air time because the person making the appearance would mention it outside the scheduled commercials.

In the Eighties there were several bars in or near the Statler Office Tower, but on Friday afternoon the staff headed to the basement to a place called Apple Annie's. A lot of people outside the staff didn't know it was there, so the Buzzards could speak freely without prying ears looking for gossip. Plus, they offered free chicken wings and great drink prices. The only drawback was there were large glass panels that looked like frosted windows. They were lit from the back so it looked like daylight. You could easily lose track of time, especially in the winter. It was like a private bar for WMMS; how did this place stay in business? It may not have needed the liquor sales. Word got around that the bar was being investigated, and the staff stayed away. True or not, Apple Annie's didn't stay open much longer after that.

In the 1980s and early 1990s, Cleveland's Flats drew tens of thousands of people every weekend, and some of the bars and restaurants had outrageous promotions to draw an early crowd. One of them was Headliners, a huge room on the east side of the Cuyahoga River that offered a twenty-five-cent happy hour. That's not a typo. It was draft beer and well liquor, but for two hours on

Friday the drinks were just a quarter. At times there were so many people you couldn't breathe—but that didn't stop the drinking! Hang your morals at the door. It's the weekend!

One thing about working for WMMS: You rarely paid for a drink. Someone was always handing you one on the house, or to say they bought one for you. Just mentioning on the air that you'd had a good time at a place would usually draw in plenty of listeners. Then there were bar tabs. Often the sales department or management would set up a tab for free drinks for the staff. That's the way it was for Coffee Break Concerts, and new staffers usually found out the hard way that a little discretion was required to get them through the day. Here's a typical example.

WMMS was breaking a lot of new acts in the Eighties and Nineties. Some, like the London Quireboys, Shaking Family, Escape Club, and others, got an artificial boost from station exposure and pretty much faded away. Others, like Tori Amos, Marc Cohn, and even Nine Inch Nails, to name a few, went on to long, successful careers. School of Fish wanted to be in that latter group. They scheduled a Coffee Break show at Peabody's, and the Buzzard bus picked up any staff member who wanted to go and dropped them off in the Flats. Guess what? Open bar for 'MMS staff, and the new folks started drinking like, well, a school of fish.

After more than a few beers, one guy discovered Grand Marnier and started knocking it back in shots. That's not something you drink in shots or after beer. After the show, the folks who didn't take the bus back decided to get some lunch at the Flat Iron Cafe. That also meant more beer, and WMMS had a tab there, too. Now, the vets on the staff knew it was probably okay to come back to work with alcohol on your breath, but you'd better not be drunk. They tried to warn the guy with the Grand Marnier, who started projectile vomiting just before he passed out. He didn't finish his lunch and slept it off in a back office when everyone returned to the station.

The 1991 Riverfest in the Flats was particularly memorable. There were record-setting crowds, and police were plenty nervous.

Working the heavy bag. "Rocco, the Rock Dog" Bennett takes a crack at the boxing equipment that hung outside the WMMS studio. The side he's punching had a caricature (by Buzzard artist David Helton) of WMJI's John Lanigan and John Webster. *Brian Chalmers*

Estimates put the Saturday attendance at a quarter million, and frankly, it was not a family event. A lot of people came early, stayed late, and were in no condition to make their own way home. Most of the folks were 'MMS fans, and the station sponsored a free show that night at the Nautica Stage with the Indigo Girls. After the show, the station took the girls and their band to dinner at Coconuts. It was supposed to be a handful of people, but word got around and every person who worked at WMMS in the Flats that night showed up, times two because they all had dates. Coconuts sealed off the deck for the Buzzards, and pretty soon drinks started flowing freely—and they weren't cheap because of River-fest! Everyone ordered food and more and more drinks, and at the end of the night the club manager grabbed the last jock standing, "Rocco, the Rock Dog," to ask who was going to cover the bill. The tab was over $5,000! Rocco scribbled a salesman's name, said 'MMS would cover it, and started wondering what he would be doing for employment the following week. That Monday, Rocco came in early and grabbed the sales guy to explain what had happened. The sales rep heard his story, smiled and shrugged. "We'll give them trade-out spots." Free commercials in exchange for a very expensive party. It was good to be king of the airwaves.

*   *   *

A personal note from Mike: I witnessed a couple of similar incidents that still seem unbelievable. The first one again involved Rocco. In 1990, St. Patrick's Day fell on a Saturday. That was a big holiday for WMMS and usually involved live remotes in morning and afternoon drive, but that wouldn't work on the weekend. The station ran a contest for a pub crawl hosted by Rocco, taking winners to five bars and then a free dinner at Cleveland's PM in the Flats. Rocco invited my designated driver, my wife Janice, and me to come along for the ride.

Everyone showed up at 11 a.m. and boarded a British double-decker bus. The promotions crew was on board, and I noticed large plastic garbage containers covered with tight lids, and boxes of WMMS shirts and giveaways from beer distributors. When the bus hit the road, they opened the containers and they were full of beer. I don't remember if they sold them, gave them away, or what, but plenty of people were drinking before we got to the first of five bars, this one in Lorain. Plans were to start out at the farthest location, spend an hour at each, and then work our way back to the Flats.

It was the middle of March, so the weather was always a crap shoot. This year we lost. It was snowing heavily, and the roads were starting to get slippery. Thankfully, none of our people were driving, especially after that first bar. They crowded in, and money and drinks started flying about wildly. After an hour, we loaded everyone back on the bus, checked their names off a list, and were on our way to the next stop.

Then it got scary.

When we got on the freeway the bus started rocking from side to side. The driver started to panic and said the riders upstairs were trying to tip the bus—and it looked like they were going to succeed! Rocco put me in charge of the downstairs group, ran upstairs, and got everything under control right away. Even so, we had four more stops, and there were a lot more guests than there were of us. Thankfully, there were no more incidents.

The second event happened a few years later, in the winter of 1996. Most of us had left WMMS after the change in ownership, but would still get together for parties and happy hours. Fagan's in the Flats was booking some name acts and had scheduled Dale Bozzio and Missing Persons for a Friday night show. The ad in *Scene* said "99 cent beers," and that along with a free concert seemed like a great combination. A dozen of us decided to meet for the show. Most of us worked downtown, so it made sense to just head there after work, which was about 6:30. I was working in television at the time and got there early to put aside some tables. I ordered a beer and the waitress said, "$3.50." Hold it! The ad said beer was 99 cents! "Oh, it is. For domestic drafts. When the band comes on it goes to five bucks." This could prove to be an expensive evening.

By that time, Rocco was already at "The End," WENZ, doing morning drive, so late nights weren't part of his routine. We all gathered and thought, "What should we do?" I happened to notice a private party in the back room and a sign that said "Media Check In." Let's see what this is all about.

It was a promotional party for the upcoming season of Sea World or Geauga Lake or something like that. I saw a huge buffet with steamship round of beef, giant piles of shrimp, steam trays galore—and a full, open bar! It took me back to my childhood in the Sixties, looking at toys in the department store, like that scene outside Higbee's in *A Christmas Story*. I asked if Rocco the Rock Dog was on the list. The person with the clip board said, "Yes. Are you him?" and I answered with a "Woof!" But wait a minute! It only said plus one. "That was a typo. It was supposed to say plus twelve!" Purgatory flashed before my eyes, but the attendant asked, "Are they here?" and all of a sudden that party got a lot more crowded.

The promotion party ended at 8 and Missing Persons wasn't going on until 10, and $5 beers weren't in the plans. A few of us gathered at one end of the bar near the stage and a barmaid came around with a round of drinks. We all went for money and she said, "You're with the WMMS group, right?" Well, we had all worked for WMMS so we said, "Yeah!" "They said to put it on the station tab. They'll sign off at the end of the night."

Station tab? Who put it on the station tab? We were the only people there who had any connection with the station.

The barmaid must have been working a day shift because she left for home right after that, but she told the person who took over we were on the tab. It was a liquid buffet!

The drinks kept flowing through the night! Rounds were sent over to folks they didn't know just to say hello. They bought so many drinks for Missing Persons that Dale Bozzio herself came over to hug everyone and say, "Thanks!" People kept tipping the help and at the end of the night the bar staff thanked everyone, said "See you soon!" and no signatures were signed.

It was one last bar tab on the Buzzard.

The Backstage Pass

Bands and Their Demands

CLEVELAND HAD A WELL earned reputation as a huge town for concerts. When rock radio was in its prime, you might have a dozen major acts come through in a week and the shows were all packed. For folks outside the industry, the backstage pass was seen as the Holy Grail, your ticket to hang out with the stars and load up on free booze, food, drugs, groupies, you name it. Nothing could be further from the truth.

It used to be a lot easier to get backstage. The Doors' Ray Manzarek remembered playing the Allen Theatre in February 1970, a matinee and an evening show. The guys in the band couldn't take the Cleveland weather, and bought heavy jackets to beat the cold. They arrived for the early show and a guy came up and said, "Welcome to Cleveland, Mr. Manzarek. May I have your coat?" "Wow!" he thought. "How cool. The folks in Cleveland have some class!" He took all their coats, the band hung out for awhile and did the show. They decided to get some dinner before the second show and asked a stage hand where the coat check guy was. "We don't have a coat check!" When that guy had said "May I have your coat," he meant it! Luckily, Bond Clothes at East Ninth and Euclid was still open and they were able to replace the coats.

Steve Sinton was one of the pioneer FM jocks at WNCR and WMMS, using the name Ginger Sutton. He said rock stars were a lot more accessible to the radio stations. The Moody Blues played Cleveland Public Hall in the early Seventies, and Sinton just casually walked backstage after the show to say hello. The band was sitting around cradling their guitars and sitting behind the drums. He said, "You guys really love the music. You can't stay away from your gear." They said that wasn't the case at all. They could see how bad security was and they were hanging on to their stuff so it wouldn't be stolen.

Sinton remembers visiting with the members of Deep Purple at Swingo's Celebrity Inn on Euclid Avenue. This was the early Seventies, and downtown was not exactly tourist friendly in those days. In fact, if you had no reason to be downtown, you stayed away for your own safety. The keyboard player Jon Lord had time to kill before the show and came walking out of his room with a purple velvet suit and matching wide-brimmed fedora. Ginger said, "Hold it! Where do you think you're going?" Lord said he was going for a walk. "Not dressed like that you're not. The pimps will think you're competition."

Backstage before a show is a busy place. If you're not working, you don't belong there. People are moving heavy equipment, there's a lot of last-minute preparations, and insurance doesn't cover people who just wander in for a good time. No one other than the band's management has access to the stars' dressing rooms (and chances are you don't want to know what's going on in there anyway!). The top acts will bring along a tour chef to feed the whole crew, but there aren't many of those. Most will have it in the contract that the promoter will serve a set number of dinners and you need a ticket to get served. The caterer charges them for every meal. Blossom Music Center has a large space backstage specifically for that purpose.

*   *   *

A personal note from Mike: I graduated from Bedford High School in 1971, and our commencement ceremony was held that June at Blossom. At the time, I never imagined I would wind up having so many profound experiences there. When I got to WMMS I had the opportunity to do a lot of side work for various publications. *Today's Rock Fax,* a radio prep service for morning drive teams, asked me to get some interview cuts with a newcomer, Sheryl Crow, and members of the Allman Brothers who were part of the HORDE tour playing Blossom. HORDE, which stood for "Horizons of Rock Developing Everywhere," offered a day-long show with a number of very different acts. Another Buzzard, John Filby, mentioned he wouldn't mind seeing the show, and we headed out to Cuyahoga Falls.

The HORDE folks treated us like celebrities. Don't get me wrong: They were getting a lot of free promotion, but they still went out of their way to make us feel welcome. We did plenty of interviews and hung out for awhile backstage. If we needed anything, we were told to just go down the corridor to the other side of the pavilion where there was a courtesy room.

As the night wore on, Filby and I decided to check out that courtesy room. It was pitch black in the corridor, and a publicist was walking along with us. Something kept brushing the tops of our heads, and suddenly the publicist yelled, "Bats!" We ducked in to the first door we came to. It went right onto the stage, and we were standing next to Gregg Allman. He did a double take, shrugged, and kept playing. Best seats in the house, even if we couldn't sit down.

My wife, Janice, and I had a similar experience when I worked at WNCX. We escorted a group of contest winners to the Who show at Gund Arena in September 2000. Someone from The Who's entourage took us through the backstage area and set us up to watch the show from the side of the stage next to the sound man. We had to stand the whole show, but we wouldn't have been sitting if they'd given us seats anyway. Part of the promotion was to feed the first two songs live to air on 'NCX. Then the sound guy would cut the feed. He probably would have done so, too—if he'd remembered. Janice and I left just before the last song (I'd seen the set list when we were onstage) to beat the traffic. We were parked close by, just down the street, and when we put on the radio we heard the end of the show!

Back to Blossom: Van Halen did a summer tour playing "sheds," open-air pavilions like Blossom, and they loved meeting the public. The bass player, Michael Anthony, was famous for heading to the

Flats when they played Cleveland and dropping a good amount of tour money for drinks with people he didn't know. I asked if there was a "meet and greet"—a carefully orchestrated visit arranged for radio people and maybe some lucky listeners where you say hello, maybe get a photo—and got the green light to bring some folks.

Van Halen was famous for its contract rider demands of "no brown M&Ms." Well, there was one other provision before we would meet the band. We were not allowed to shake Eddie Van Halen's hand. He wasn't a germ freak or anything like that. His wedding ring was on his pick hand and he didn't want to bruise his fingers from a tight handshake. You couldn't ask for nicer guys.

And now we come to KISS. They were doing a double-headliner tour with Aerosmith, with each band taking turns opening for the other on alternate nights. I was doing a video taping for a broadcasters' event and called KISS management to see if they would do a quick testimonial for Kid Leo and Denny Sanders. They switched me over to Frank DiLeo, a former Clevelander who had also been one of Michael Jackson's managers. This time around he was working with KISS. "Sure. I'll leave passes for you and the camera guy at the booth."

Aerosmith was opening that night at Blossom, and DiLeo had me sit in a backstage lounge. Gene Simmons arrived first, in full costume. "I'm Gene. You here for the taping?" Yeah, I'll keep it quick. Out of nowhere he says, "You ever been to Hershey, Pennsylvania? We were there last night. Disaster. There were cables all over the stage, almost tripped a few times, and a rocket almost flew up my ass." He closed his eyes and slowly shook his head. "I will not return. Would you care for some cheese?" The rest of the band showed up, we did the taping and as we left we heard Simmons complaining about, "Blah blah blah and I'm not seeing a dime from it."

*   *   *

When Aerosmith played the Richfield Coliseum on their "Get a Grip" tour in August, 1993, they hosted the WMMS staff and some listeners backstage before the show. They were very gracious, posing for photos and signing autographs, but Steven Tyler had one condition: He had to personalize the signature or he wouldn't sign. Even in the days before eBay there was a huge secondary market for rock star signatures. Personalized signatures cut the price down considerably.

George Thorogood, Alice Cooper, and Greg Lake of Emerson, Lake and Palmer have always been very generous with their fans. Thorogood would make it a point to catch an Indians game at Municipal Stadium when he was in town, and you almost always saw Cooper on a local golf course when he came through Cleveland. All were very approachable. It was tough to get to David Bowie; for many years the only people he would allow backstage were the *Plain Dealer*'s Jane Scott and anyone from WMMS who did the pre-show interview.

Robert Plant agreed to meet groups of fans in a WMMS promotion when he did a solo show a Public Hall in November 1993. A few minutes before the show, there were two groups off to the side of the stage. Plant came out, posed with the first group, and spotted Jane Scott. He'd known Jane for 25 years, and spent the rest of the time talking to her until the first notes from his band and he raced onstage. The other group got a good look, a quick hello, but no photo.

Brian May of Queen started a solo career for a time when Queen disbanded after Freddie Mercury's death. His band opened for Guns N' Roses on their 1993 tour, and he agreed to headline a show at the Agora honoring WMMS on its twenty-fifth anniversary. He visited the station and invited everyone to stop by after the show that night. Here's the remarkable thing about May: He remembered every show he did in Cleveland. Brian May is a brilliant guy. He has a Ph.D. in astrophysics and a mind like a steel trap. He remembered how hard the stage was at Music Hall in 1975, and that the 1976 concert was on Valentine's Day. He also recalled that Freddie loved the crowd at the Richfield Coliseum in 1982. An amazing talent with an equally remarkable memory!

Backstage is not necessarily the best place to get interviews. It's usually way too busy before, and after, people are anxious to get to the post-show party or back to the hotel. The studio is the ideal location, and Denny Sanders had plenty of opportunities at WMMS. He offered to give "a snapshot" of his personal experiences.

Among the best, of course, would be his phone interview with John Lennon. "This is probably my most famous interview," Sanders says, "and, although I only spoke with him on the phone, I found him warm, witty and forthcoming. Not at all the edgy guy that I was expecting." Lennon even improvised a joke about Cleveland when he said goodbye.

Then there was Brian Wilson of the Beach Boys. "He came by as a surprise guest with Mike Love," Sanders says, "and the less said about Mike Love the better. At the time, the early Eighties, it was reported that Brian Wilson was pretty out of it. But although somewhat shaky, he was able to engage nicely and gave a great interview. I don't remember many of the questions since this was a compete surprise. I just ad-libbed as best that I could. I do remember one exchange: I said, 'I've read that you have a piano in a large box of sand to get you in the mood for composing. Is true or just an urban legend?' Brian said, 'I used to. But the cats got into it, so I took it out.'"

The rest of the interview is long gone, Sanders said. "The WMMS general manager at the time was a real Beach Boys fan and borrowed the tape of the live broadcast from me right after the interview concluded, never returned it, and reportedly lost it. (Radio Rule Number One: Never lend a master tape to anyone)."

Sanders had more to say about the Beach Boys.

"Carl Wilson was on my show after their performance, I believe at the World Series of Rock. Dennis Wilson had run away with Murray Saul someplace (God help us) and Carl went on the air with something like, 'Dennis, if you are listening, come back. We have a plane to catch.' I also remember asking Carl if he ever heard The Euclid Beach Band's record *No Surf In Cleveland*. He didn't.

I played it and he loved it. We joked that since Eric Carmen of the Raspberries produced the record, the act should have been called 'The Beach Berries.'"

Another highlight was Mama Cass of the Mamas and the Papas. "What a sweetheart! One of my best interviews. Warm and friendly. I remember that she had pretty rotten teeth, though." Thankfully it didn't affect her voice.

Some had an image that didn't reflect their intellect. Sanders recalls, "I interviewed Joey and Johnny Ramone, and they were smart and articulate. I always got a kick out of The Ramones, but after the interview, my respect level for them went way up." Bob Seger was special as well. "Love him," Sanders says. "Like interviewing the guy that drives the beer truck, and I mean that in a nice way. Probably the least pretentious rock star that I ever talked to."

Suzi Quatro showed amazing potential as well, according to Sanders.

"Great gal. Should have been as big as Joan Jett in the U.S.A., but big in the U.K. Great interview. I did her on TV once [you have a dirty mind, dear reader] and also put together a TV commercial for WMMS featuring her. The commercial was never completed and never aired because we shot it at Channel 3, which was owned by NBC in those days and the unions were pretty strict. We ran out of time on the session when it took a half hour to find a union guy to move a stepladder out of the shot."

Not to mention that the lavalier mic that hung around her neck caused the noise of unzipping her top to show a WMMS t-shirt to sound like a buzz saw.

What about Gene Simmons of Kiss? "Did him on TV, too [will you STOP it!]. This was in the late Seventies and he wasn't quite the egotist that he later became, so he was a lot less guarded in our conversation. He was a Marvel comic fan, so I arranged that the interview be shot at Cosmic Comics down at the Colonial Arcade, and I believe that he ended up buying some rare stuff from a very pleased owner, Tony Isabella."

A few years later, Sanders got a chance to interview a longtime

The Buzzard's "Matt the Cat" Lapczynski (left) may hold the record for hosting rock shows in Northeast Ohio. He introduced hundreds of acts for the weekly "Coffeebreak Concert" broadcast from the Cleveland Agora. He's seen here with Peter Frampton. *Brian Chalmers*

favorite, Ronnie Spector. "How do you interview someone who you were in love with since you were a teenager?" he asks. "In the interview, she revealed to me that it wasn't just guys who wrote love letters to The Ronettes! One sad note: We had her for a WMJI Moondog Coronation Ball show in the Nineties, and we tried to book her on one of those local TV chat shows for publicity the day before. The TV producer called me back and said that she was going to pass because she never heard of her or The Ronettes and neither had anyone on the production staff. Time waits for no one."

Disc jockeys become historians in so many ways, though some of the people making that history didn't always co-operate.

On the down side was Captain Beefheart. Does Denny Sanders remember Beefheart? You better believe it. "This was way back in 1972. The good Captain was attempting to get a bit more mainstream, so he released the album *Clear Spot* on Warner Brothers Records. At that time, WMMS had another album station against us called WNCR. WMMS was playing the *Clear Spot* album and WNCR was not. The Warner Brothers promotional representative pitched me an in-studio interview with Captain Beefheart, and I jumped at it. I thought he was a fascinating artist. However, I told the promo man that I didn't want to do much of an interview, but rather have him play DJ and present some of his favorite things. He could have his run of the library. I found that when you have really off-the-wall people like Beefheart, it is best not to try to do much Q&A because they like to remain mysterious and elusive. Or maybe they just can't talk with the same creativity and authority as their recordings. Anyway, the promo guy thought it was a great idea. The day of the interview, I'm driving to the studio and I hear WNCR announce that Captain Beefheart will be arriving at any minute and will be playing DJ! This is from the station that never played his new album! When the promo guy shows up at my studio, I tell him that the interview is cancelled. The promo guy goes to tell Beefheart, who barges into the studio ranting that he has never been cancelled in his life. I told him that his dumb promo guy stole my idea, gave it to my competitor, which is not even playing your album like we are, and brought you over there first. Beefheart says that he does not care about that. He thunders 'I'm going to ruin you in the business' and storms out."

Looking back, Sanders believes "this may explain why the record industry's attempts at marketing and promoting Captain Beefheart were futile!"

Sometimes artists remake themselves. Lou Reed was in that number. "During the *Sally Can't Dance* period, he came to town with the short, dyed-blond hair and black leather outfit," Sanders recalls. "We went to get him at Hopkins Airport. He emerges from the arrival gate door and hocks a big loogie right on the floor. (Am I dating myself? Spits a big one.) Then we ride back to the city in a limo. WMMS was tuned in and we were playing something from Roy Wood's band, Wizzard. He was critiquing the song, saying that they should have a sax break here, etc., etc. Then he bitched about the next song. And the next. He arrived at the station to be interviewed by Kid Leo."

Leo had a reputation for not suffering any bullshit. As Sanders recalls, "Leo opened the interview with, 'Hey, Lou, is it true that blondes have more fun?' Great line. Lou was in no mood for fun. I believe he uttered an obscenity and was a jerk through the rest of the interview. Then we went to some place with a bunch of tables so some of the local press could attempt to talk to him. There was a lull in the questions, so I asked him what he thought of Television, Tom Verlaine's group, who obviously were inspired by the Velvets and Reed. He looked at me and said 'I don't watch television!' Thinking that he misunderstood, I said 'No, Tom Verlaine's band'. He repeated, this time more sternly, 'I said I never watch television'.

"Some writer from one of those little punk rock rags was sitting next to me. A couple of weeks later, I read in his magazine that 'a clueless Denny Sanders of WMMS kept asking Lou what his favorite television shows were.' Thanks a lot, kid. Great reporting."

Sanders remembers Reed's return trip in 1984.

"Reed agreed to play a Coffee Break Concert for the station. I produced and directed the show at the time, and prepared myself and host Matt the Cat for the worst. But this was a different Lou. Gone was the somewhat pathetic hip act, replaced by a guy in a sweater with wire rims who looked more like a college professor than a rock star. He did a knockout performance to a very appreciative crowd, loaded with heartfelt 'thank yous.' He was respectful of Matt during the interview periods, and after the broadcast actually thanked me! Either he grew up a little in the intervening years, was running out of money and needed to quit alienating people, or both. Regardless of the reason, it was nice to see the real artist come through without all the packaging."

Not all the Coffee Break Concerts were as successful. The group UFO stands out in Sanders's memory.

"Now, the show was live at 1 p.m., and the act sometimes arrived

Don't be nervous—it's only about 80,000 people! Michael Stanley shares a few words with WMMS's John Gorman and "Kid Leo" Travagliante before the Michael Stanley Band's record breaking run at Blossom Music Center in 1982. *Janet Macoska*

in town as late as that morning. Around 9 we got a report that their plane was delayed, but they should arrive in time. When it was obvious that the plane was delayed further and not going to make it, we rescheduled the show and put a re-run on the air. Unfortunately, the audience was already in place at the Agora for the live broadcast. Well, guess who had to go on stage and explain what happened! Even though we had presented dozens of live broadcasts featuring major artists with never an admission charge, as I started to explain that UFO's plane was delayed due to bad weather at their location, the crowd turned ugly. People yelled 'Bullshit! Bullshit! Bullshit!' in unison, and I was accosted on the way out by several people who accused me and the station of lying about having arranged UFO for a Coffee Break in the first place. UFO did come back a few weeks later, and played the show, but that day was a vivid illustration of how quickly people can turn against something or somebody, especially when in a mob mentality."

And now we come to a group that didn't help itself with their golden opportunity to do a Coffee Break.

"Do you remember a band called Big Country?" Sanders asks. "Well, you're not alone, because they are pretty much forgotten today. But back in the early Eighties, this Scottish group showed great promise with their first album, so we booked them on a Coffee Break Concert. The live broadcast began at 1 p.m. Suddenly, after maybe one or two songs, the lead singer says something like, 'I'm sorry, we can't carry on,' and the band walked off the stage! Matt grabs the mic and immediately throws it back to the station. Just one problem: Since we were a 24/7/365 station, we used that hour to disassemble and clean the main studio's console, so the board was in pieces when we heard this surprise. They scrambled to patch over to another studio back at the station, but it took several minutes and we were in dead air all that time. It turns out that the members of Big Country were all big boozers and were so hung over that they couldn't play. They broke up soon after. Gosh, I wonder why."

Engineer Frank Foti remembers the Big Country show—or no show—well. "That was the one time every week [engineers] could get in the studio and not be in the way," he says. "Well, we were finally going to install the new furniture and equipment in the 'MMS air studio. We went to the remote feed [from the Agora] with the idea that while the concert was on the air that would give us the opportunity to get one of the auxiliary studios up and ready. While all that was going on, they found out the show ended abruptly and we had to go back! But we had crossed the point of no return. Everything was turned off, disconnected, and if we tried to go on the air it would have been dead air for quite awhile."

Red flags went up at the station all at once. It was a time to make some quick decisions because WMMS off the air was simply not acceptable.

"Luckily, we were able to quickly get something on the air from a back production room," Foti recalls. It minimized any weirdness on the radio when those things happened. Over the years there had been a few and there definitely is some scrambling going on behind the scenes.

Even so, management wanted answers. Kid Leo was management, and if he was mad, you knew it. Usually that meant *everyone* knew it.

"In fairness to Leo, someone who passionately cared about what went on the radio and how it went on the radio, let's just say the things he said in the hallway would not have been allowed on the air by the Federal Communications Commission," according to Foti. "They would not have been happy if that had been on the radio." But it was fueled more by concern than anger, and he could cool down just as quickly.

Denny Sanders adds, "You will find some of the Coffee Breaks posted online. The Lou Reed Show is there, and so are shows by INXS, John Mellencamp, Foghat, Bryan Adams, Peter Frampton, Cyndi Lauper, The Romantics, Artful Dodger, and a host of others, as well as some of the early studio shows featuring people like Warren Zevon, Tom Waits, and Kenny Loggins. However, no one has posted the Big Country show." It would be a very short clip.

*   *   *

A personal note from Mike: Let me end this chapter with a story about the Richfield Coliseum—that happened in New York City. Our old friend Andy Oeftering (you remember him from his dealings with Count Manolesco at WERE) had moved to the East Village, and in October 1982 we decided to pay him a visit. We ended up that evening at the St. Mark's Bar, the same tavern seen in the Rolling Stones video "Waiting on a Friend." The video begins with Mick Jagger standing on the steps of a building down the street and then meeting Keith Richards. (That same building was used on the cover of Led Zeppelin's *Physical Graffiti* album.) They meet up with the rest of the band and perform on stage at the St. Mark's Bar.

It was a slow night with maybe a handful of people and, sure enough, there was that same tiny stage at the far end of the room.

As luck would have it, we sat next to a guy from the Stones' stage crew who must have had two dozen backstage laminates in his jacket pockets. We all put down a lot of beers, and he told us what it was like to travel with the Stones. You worked four weeks straight, setting up the show in one city while the band played in another the night before. It was hard work, but Keith Richards himself would often come back to check if everyone was fed and if they needed anything. Then they would fly you back home, wherever home was, for some R&R with your family. This could go on for a couple years. Absolutely no drugs or alcohol, but at the end of the tour the band would fly your family to a special concert just for them with a full spread of food and a fully stocked open bar. They'd have it at a place with a huge ballroom, and the party would go on until the wee hours. Then he asked where we were from? "Oh, we're from Cleveland."

His eyebrows shot up into his scalp. "Richfield Coliseum! Worst dates on the tour! Somebody had a private party going on backstage when we were there. The Stones threatened to cancel the second show unless everyone was out!"

The band had played a two-night stand at the Coliseum the previous November. We ended up closing the bar, shaking hands and hailing taxis. Fascinating guy, but I think his story had some holes.

First of all, Belkin Productions always ran a tight ship. Nice guys, but they had a business to run and they wouldn't risk damaging their reputation or the band's safety by allowing a crowd backstage. Plus, the Stones security controlled all backstage access. You had to be pretty important to get an all-access laminate or cloth backstage pass, and no pass, no access. You didn't want to mess with their security. Friendly, but firm—and if you wanted to give them a hard time there was one hand on the back of your pants, one on your collar and it's time for your flying lesson. But here's the point: He may have confused the event, but he knew the city and the arena, and if you didn't belong backstage it was best to stay in your seat.

"There's evil in this building"

WERE and Adventures in Talk Radio

HERE'S ONE THAT REALLY hit home. There's no other way to tell it other than through an eyewitness account. At times, it may cross the line of good taste. If you're easily offended, this may not be the chapter for you.

When WERE switched from all-news to news-and-talk there was a big push to get compelling guests on the air. I worked evenings one week with Don Robertson, who carried a lot of weight thanks to his column in the *Cleveland Press*. That was some week! One night his guest was Jesse Owens, who had brought so much attention to Cleveland after he embarrassed Nazi Germany with his four gold medals at the 1936 Olympics in Berlin. He stopped by the station to promote Greyhound Package Express, and was bigger and older, but you knew you were in the presence of greatness. Robertson had a unique delivery, and he marched in to say, "Now listen, *Olshevsky*, I need you to keep Mr. Owens entertained until I'm ready to have him on. Fifteen, twenty minutes. Go." Like he had to ask me twice!

Two surprising things about that conversation. First, Owens smoked. I guess he wasn't running track anymore, which brings me to the second point. We were having a very friendly chat, and I mentioned, "That must have been something to see Hitler storm out of the stadium after you won those medals." Owens flicked the ash of his cigarette and said, "You know what? I don't think that happened. Somebody pointed him out during the opening ceremonies, but he was way off in the distance. I just saw this tiny little figure." He went on to say that Hitler only wanted to give medals to the German athletes. "I heard he never came back. I didn't see him after the opening parade." Owens said he never heard that Hitler left after his race until well after, and figured it was U.S. propaganda—which was okay by him.

A couple of nights later, Robertson was angry. Senator Ted Kennedy was coming to town, and Robertson wanted him on his show. The person who could make that happen was Senator Howard Metzenbaum, who was a friend of Robertson, but you wouldn't know it by their exchange that evening. Robertson had to go on the air, and he told me to let him know when Metzenbaum called. Sure enough, he called the newsroom, and I put him through when Robertson went to the network news. I could hear down the hall that the conversation wasn't going well.

Robertson put Metzenbaum on hold and buzzed the newsroom. He was playing some spots and told me, "He says Kennedy doesn't have time for my show! You tell that son of a bitch—" *Right, Don. I'll say it just like that.* I got on the phone and said, "Don would really like Senator Kennedy on his show. It's really important to him." Metzenbaum snapped, "I told him to forget it! You tell that—" I ran back and forth for close to half an hour, cleaning up the language from both of them. Finally, Robertson got off the air, slammed the production door closed, and the conversation took an ugly tone.

A few days after that, Ted Kennedy walked into the studio.

WERE was a postage stamp of a station, but it still had some pull when it came to booking guests. On any given day you might see Cesar Chavez pass you in the men's room, hear Bob Hope calling the studio about his days in Cleveland, or see Connie Stevens walking down to the hall to the air studio. These were big names back then.

Some guests made you nervous. Let me give you some background.

WERE was not an especially nice place to work. The place was held together with chewing gum and rubber bands, and the equipment was badly outdated and in need of repair. The engineers must have had magic wands, because no one could figure out how they kept stuff operating. At one time there was a computer called the RA-10 that was like HAL in *2001: A Space Odyssey*. It was racks of computer carts, and out of nowhere it would cut the mikes and start playing spots at random. The station hired a consultant who refused to start work until it was dismantled and on the curb.

We used to joke that the call letters should be pronounced "weary." When someone got fired, other employees got angry— because they were envious. "Dammit! Why couldn't it be me!" The one thing that kept people there was the AFTRA union contract, which offered incentives for people there for the long haul. I was there for nine and a half years, and we all knew we were wasting our time. But I also had four weeks vacation, and all my holidays off. I'd lose that at a new job so. A lot of the staff just soldiered on.

We had a solid union president with Ken Bichl. I came from a family that was fiercely pro-union. I used to joke with my uncles that our family motto should be "Union man. Company boy." We wouldn't even eat Payday candy bars because they came from a non-union shop. But I also thought that you only needed a union at a radio station if you *really* needed one—and WERE really needed one.

When new owners came in with a broom in 1986, a lot of loyal union people were the first to go and, luckily, I was one of them. I had almost a whole year's severance coming, and was rubbing my hands to get that check. There was one hitch. They wouldn't hand it over until I signed a waiver, and I wasn't signing anything. I called Ken Bichl, and he got the new management on the phone to explain what they owed in the contract, and some additional compensation they forgot about. They said, "We don't read it that way," and Bichl said "Tough. That's the way it's written. You've got twenty-four hours." It didn't take that long. There was a knock on the door the next morning with a check for the full amount.

Now, here's the rub. The new owners only had so much money, and they couldn't afford to pay everyone's severance. The jocks at WGCL were all shown the door, and they had to make good on some big contracts. Some had to be kept on in minor jobs with major salaries.

Let's go back to before the sale. John Webster is best known for his time with John Lanigan at WMJI, but he also did a couple of stints at WERE. He was also interested in astrology and the paranormal. One Saturday, Webster walked into the side door with a friend who was a psychic. As soon as they walked in the door, the psychic grabbed Webster's arm and said, "There's evil in this building!" Webster didn't blink. "That's the management. They're not here on weekends."

One program director had the long-standing nickname of "Iscariot," and while the "suits" were singing the blues about not being able to sell time on the station, they were always telling the air staff to keep it short to fit in all the spots. Here's why: If you looked at the station's commercial logs, there would be entries with a code that said "T" or "TR." That meant they were trade-outs, air time traded for products or services. There were trade-outs with boat and car dealers, home improvement stores and a garden center. Lots of trade-outs. The news cars were rolling wrecks and dangerous, we had no use for a "news boat," and the only shrubbery we had was a bush in a planter outside the front door that bums peed in overnight. There was something fishy . . . and it wasn't just that stupid bush. A few years later, the IRS walked into the comptroller's office and said they would need several years' worth of records and the conference room. Word got around the industry that at least one person "paid" for his sins.

It was just a weird atmosphere working there. Remember that building in the movie *Ghostbusters*, where the gatekeeper Zuul plans to bring forth the demon Gozer? We were pretty sure when Armageddon came, the opposing team would be coming out WERE's front door. We didn't expect the advance team to walk through the news room—but he did.

The WERE newsroom was a very busy place during drive times. It was like shoveling coal into a steam engine on a speeding train or feeding a hungry monster. We hit the ground running, and we didn't stop. We used to joke that we didn't have time to break wind. Not that anyone would have noticed. Back in 1979, a lot of people smoked cigarettes in the studio and the newsroom, and Casey Coleman and I smoked cigars. When there was a full house, there was a thick haze across the second floor.

Busy or not, you still had to answer phones. One day I was racing against the clock, as usual, beating on a typewriter, when I heard a promo for Larry Morrow's talk show at 10 a.m. His special guest later that day was from *Saturday Night Live*, Michael O'Donoghue.

Whoa! Who did he say? No! Before I could get out of my seat to check the spot the phone rang. It was Sally Lewis. She had no reason to listen to WERE except to hear if it was still on the air, but sure enough, she'd heard it, too.

"Please say I didn't hear what I think I did?" Afraid so! Her voice took on an urgent tone. "We have to stop this!"

Here's why.

Michael O'Donoghue was a brilliant writer and, most likely, the antichrist. Some of his early work in *National Lampoon* magazine centered on Nazis and fetish wear for children, and it degenerated from there. When he switched over to *SNL* he was seen in the very first skit in 1975 teaching English to John Belushi as a foreigner saying, "I would like to feed your fingertips to the wolverines," and clutching his chest to fall dead from a heart attack. He demonstrated what it might look like if steel knitting needles were thrust into Mike Douglas' eyes.

O'Donoghue openly mocked the writers and cast members. "This script is brilliant!" he'd say, and toss it right in the trash. Garrett Morris said O'Donoghue's abuse drove him to drugs, and *SCTV*'s Catherine O'Hara quit the cast before her first show so she wouldn't have to deal with him. Clearly, broadcast standards meant nothing to Michael O'Donoghue—and he would be broadcasting that day on WERE! He had to be stopped.

Anyone who knows Larry Morrow will tell you he's the same off the air as when he's in the studio. He's a kind, warm, generous person with a calming effect on anyone he speaks to. Larry Morrow is seen to this day as a genuinely wonderful guy—the polar opposite of his guest that morning. I grabbed him as soon as he came in door. Maybe I was a little frantic but I think I had reason to be. "Larry! This guy is bad juju! A horrible, terrible person!" I ran down a litany of his career low lights, and Morrow smiled. He grabbed my arm, smiled and said, "Mike. We're going to be fine."

Hey. I tried.

About twenty minutes before showtime O'Donoghue walked through the haze of newsroom smoke, and he looked mean. Real mean! He was there to promote the videocassette release for his film *Mr. Mike's Mondo Video*, which was also being shown that night at the Village Theater in Orange. The film was an extension of his *SNL* work. Dan Ackroyd poked his webbed toes with a screwdriver. There's a scene where Sid Vicious from the Sex Pistols sings Sinatra's "My Way" and shoots a handgun into the audience. Vicious would die a few months later from a heroin overdose after killing his girlfriend. (Honda would later use that same version of the song in its TV ad for the Acura TLX. Times change!)

The show started and although there were a few comments that made me wince, O'Donoghue was pretty well behaved. There was a giant sigh of relief. A couple of minutes after, Morrow walked into the newsroom and asked me to come with him. We walked into the conference room and there was O'Donoghue. "Michael O, meet Michael O!" O'Donoghue shook my hand and said, "Hello, Mike. Larry said some very nice things about you!" We had a picture taken and he walked back through the newsroom to the lobby.

O'Donoghue was not the same guy I expected, but the camera doesn't lie. When the photo came back he wasn't the person who shook my hand. The sinister quality jumped off the page.

Most of the radio guests I had contact with were usually very gracious. After all, they're at the station to promote something. A couple of names from the World Wrestling Federation, Jimmy "The Mouth of the South" Hart and Bobby "The Brain" Heenan, couldn't have been friendlier. They stopped by WMMS, joked and chatted with everyone that came in the lunchroom, and Heenan even made coffee after he poured the last cup. It came up that Hart was a member of The Gentrys, the band that had a hit with "I Keep on Dancin.'" But when they went on with the Morning Zoo—bang! They turned into "pro rasslers," and were entertaining in a whole different way.

Rock stars could pose some minor problems, but most were pretty easy to deal with. Back in the early days of WMMS, Neil Young stopped by the station for a chat with Billy Bass and got into a heated discussion with one of the newsroom folks who walked into the production studio. The newsroom guy made it clear he didn't care for rock music, Young mocked him for wearing a tie, and the news guy criticized Young's new bell bottoms, which he'd bought a few days before in New York. The newsie said he'd worn them in the Navy and didn't miss them. Thankfully, the folks at WHK were rarely asked to help out with WMMS interviews.

"Good line, smart ass"

In-Studio Guests

IN STUDIO GUESTS CAN be unpredictable, and sometimes they can have more demands than a backstage concert rider. When Todd Rundgren visited the Buzzard Morning Zoo he insisted on being called "TR-i," which stood for "Todd Rundgren Interactive." He was plugging *No World Order*, one of the first download albums, and would only sign autographs on that tour as "TR-i."

Def Leppard wanted to premier songs from their new album on a promotional tour through Cleveland, but only if they did so with the guys on the 'MMS morning show. Problem was, they were coming through on Saturday, and Jeff and Flash had weekends off. Needless to say the folks in radio land got a little surprise that weekend. The clock radio went off and they probably wondered what day it was.

When David Crosby came by to talk to Ruby Cheeks about his autobiography, he would only do the interview if she promised not to mention Woodstock. When I was at WNCX we did quite a few phone interviews, and there were similar stories. John Fogerty didn't want to be asked about Creedence Clearwater Revival, Gene Simmons of KISS nixed any talk about marriage, and Bryan Ferry made it clear he would not comment about a recent controversy where he wore something that looked like a Nazi outfit on stage. And at 'MMS, Len Goldberg found out the hard way that Slash didn't follow instructions well.

Guns N' Roses were in town for a show at the Richfield Coliseum. They were one of the hottest acts on the road, and their reputations preceded them. Sometimes they would start their shows three to four hours late, and that was more than just an

Comedy great Sam Kinison loved WMMS and made it a point to stop by the Buzzard Morning Zoo to trade lines with Mr. Leonard. It was also no secret that Kinison had plenty of help staying awake all night, none of it legal. *Brian Chalmers*

inconvenience for the audience. Promoters would often get stuck paying huge penalty fees and overtime to everyone from stage-hands to security when the shows went past the arranged times. Ticket sales were dragging, and the band's management arranged to have Slash call Len "The Boom" Goldberg, who was filling in on afternoon drive. He told Slash before they went on the air to watch his language because the station didn't need any headaches from the FCC. "Yeah, I'm cool. I'm cool," Slash promised.

Goldberg asked some pretty good questions, some Slash wanted to answer and some that he just blew off. At the end of the conver-sation Boom asked if Slash had any last words for Cleveland. He yelled, "Yeah! Get your shit together and come out to the show." Boom cut the mikes, went to a song and Slash said, "Hey man. I'm sorry, I—" Slash found out Boom could be just as intimidating on the phone as he was in person! He used most of the words he asked

Slash not to use, and in very creative ways, before he slammed down the receiver.

Most of the comedy clubs would make the rounds of Friday morning radio with their headliners for that weekend. Some of these comics would have had only get a couple hours' sleep after the previous night's show, so you really didn't expect many to come in and "make funny." The routine was they would stop by the station, yawn a few times, tell a few jokes from their acts, "Go see them tonight at the Tee Hee Hut," and go to breakfast. Sam Kinison, however, could come in and tear the place up. He wouldn't go to bed after his show the night before, and that probably wasn't coffee that was keeping him awake! He was an amazing talent who would pose for any photo and would never turn down a request for an autograph. You could add Judy Tenuta to that list.

Another guy who never slowed down was Bobby Slayton. They call him "The Pitbull of Comedy" and "Yid Vicious." A hundred miles an hour and drop-dead funny, and the only guy I ever heard keep up with him was John Lanigan, who can improvise with the best. He and Slayton became fast friends.

Not all the comics came off that well.

When Ed Ferenc went on vacation at WMMS, I would fill in on the zoo, and Flash had a lot of vacation. If Jeff Kinzbach was off the same week they would pair me up with Ric Bennett, better known as "Rocco, the Rock Dog," or Lisa Dillon. Once Jeff and Flash were both off at the same time, but Rocco had his hands full moving us from the Statler Office Tower to the Avenue at Tower City, and I believe Lisa was on maternity leave, so I ended up that week with Laura Farrell. Pat Artl was producing the show and even running the control board, and the week went by pretty quick. Friday came up before we knew it, and we were all looking forward to the weekend. Then it was time for the comedian.

I don't remember her name. She called herself "The Madame of Comedy," and before we went on, Laura asked what she wanted to talk about. She smiled and said, "My whole act is how much I hate men!"

Let's review. In the studio we have Laura and the alleged comedian. Artl always had ten things going at once, and his job was like conducting an orchestra. I was on my own, but I figured a few embarrassing minutes from now it would be over. Nothing against this woman. She was actually pretty nice. Not really funny, but nice enough when the mikes were off. I don't think she went on to have much of a career because I Googled her when I was fact-checking the book and couldn't find any mention of her name. Plus, I'm just not into so-called humor that targets individuals unless it's self-effacing. We talked on the air a bit and Laura said, "Hey, let's hear some of your act." The Madame didn't blink. "I've got one for each of you! Laura, are you gay?" Laura said no, and the Madame said, "Me neither—but I'd do you!" Then she looked over at me.

"Mike, what do you call your penis?" Don't do this. I'm in no mood. "Well?"

I said, "I don't have to call it. I drag it along with me."

Her eyebrows shot into her scalp, Artl buckled at the knees, and Laura wisely cut in and said, "Check out the Madame of Comedy all this weekend at Uncle Yuk Yuks," or wherever she was booked. The mikes were off and the Madame said, "Good line, smart ass." I was pretty sure I was going to get called to the other side of the building, but the only comments came from listeners and they were all good. I walked the Madame out to the lobby to meet her driver. She shook my hand and said, "This was fun! Let's do it again. Next time I come through I'll call you." She never called me, or any part of me, after that.

Theater of the Mind

The Crystal Ballroom, a Phony Funeral,
and a Trip to Celebrity Donuts

RADIO IS BEST WHEN you can visualize what's happening. We've already discussed what Orson Welles did with the Mercury Theater, but a lot of local radio people also staged events, and some really knew how to pull it off.

Music stations were famous for phony rock festivals. In the early Seventies, WNOB-FM in Newbury had a syndicated special called The Ultimate Rock Concert with Brother John Rydgren introducing records and doing stage announcements against the sound of a crowd, with Bob Lewis, "Baba Lou," cutting in with backstage interviews. Dia Stein really knew her way around the WMMS production studio and put together similar shows like Buzzard Fest and Camp Buzzard, which was aimed at promoting a special WMMS clothing line at the May Company.

John Rio, better known as Mr. Leonard, would play live recordings on the Morning Zoo that he supposedly recorded on stage at local clubs the night before, and once promised he would bungee jump off the Terminal Tower. Here's the problem: WMMS, and especially Mr. Leonard, were incredibly popular, and on the appointed day a huge crowd clogged up Public Square. They did the jump live in the studio against sound effects, and the switchboard lit up asking where Mr. Leonard was. He just said he did it on the other side of the building so he could look at the secretaries in the lawyers' offices.

WMMS also performed its own contemporary version of the *War of the Worlds* for the crowd that provided their own pharmaceutically generated special effects. WCLV did too, a few decades later, featuring local media celebrities and politicians. The driving force behind that production was the mega-talented Jim Mehrling, who a few years back produced nightly vignettes introducing his nightly World of Entertainment show on WERE.

Over the years, and despite the fact that WERE stressed the credibility of its news department, the station staged a good amount of special programming. Back in the mid-1970s, the entire news staff, including Peter Wellish and a young Carl Monday, reported from a phony funeral route for Gary Dee, who would lie in state on Public Square. The live broadcast included remarks by People Power talk show host Merle Pollis and a eulogy by Count John Manolesco, who described the entire event as "A travesty! A mockery!" At that point, Gary Dee peeked out of his casket to loudly heckle "Count Phony Baloney! Hey Doctor Voodoo!"

When WERE had its news and talk format in the 1980s, the reporters put together a phony St. Patrick's Day parade a couple of years in a row that ran in morning drive. Problem was, people thought it was a real parade and started calling at 7 a.m. asking what streets to avoid.

And, of course, Ray Hoffman's Sunday show was like an audio acid trip for the upper demos. He would occasionally take the show "on the road," broadcasting live from the imaginary Celebrity Donuts shop located on Doan Court in downtown Cleveland. Of course, if you know the downtown area, it's an alley that at the time was behind the Trailways bus station. These were the days before Google maps, so calls would come in asking where the most ornate donut house in the city was located so they could take out-of-town guests. Sometimes Hoffman would tape interviews with guests during the week and play them against the Celebrity Donuts sound effects so it sounded like they were at the remote!

But the one guy who performed theater of the mind longer and better than anyone is pretty much forgotten today.

Wayne Mack was one of the old timers who held on right into the 1990s. Every week starting in the early 1950s, he would broadcast on WDOK-AM from "the balcony radio box at the Waltz

Palace, overlooking the great glistening dance floor and the huge stage" at "Northern Ohio's oldest and most beautiful ballroom." He said the ballroom was easy to get to, right on the lakefront, just "twenty-two miles outside the city on picturesque Sunset Road." He encouraged people to come out "tonight if you can" to join hundreds of other couples who were already there and had been coming since it opened in 1921. It wasn't just the house band either. Some of the biggest names in music would stop in and show the crowd what they could do. But the ballroom was actually between your ears, created with a microphone and a handful of records. Mack had plenty of practice. He had done it so often, and did it so easily that you'd swear he was broadcasting from a big band show. The ballroom had "sparkling chandeliers and red carpeting" and was full of what my grandmother would call "rich society babas" heading out to swanky private parties after a night on the town.

The reason this bit came off so well week after week is that a lot of stations really did broadcast from big dance halls. WHK would air shows from the Glens Pavilion in Bedford, and you'd hear other broadcasts from Geauga Lake, and just about any place with a stage. Bill Randle, Phil McLean, and Bob West would do live jazz shows from clubs and theaters around the city. Still, Mack did it so convincingly that you had to wonder if he really did think he was at the Waltz Palace.

Keep in mind that this was broadcast on the AM band. Most of the audience back then didn't know or even care that FM existed. AM stations that had FM outlets pretty much just simulcast what was on the AM band. Here's an example. WERE-FM was at 98.5, and in 1953 the management was thinking about putting on different programming. That December, the station started airing an announcement asking if anyone was out there. It said, "If you can hear this announcement, you are listening to WERE-FM. We beg your pardon for interrupting this program momentarily. This is Ed Stevens, the program director of WERE. We are considering the broadcast of some FM-only programming. However, before we can

WDOK's Wayne Mack was so convincing in describing his make-believe band concerts that people would drive around for hours looking for the ballroom.
Cleveland Public Library

do this it's necessary to measure in some way the number of people who listen. We would appreciate a card or letter from you if this announcement is coming into your home, stating simply, 'I heard the FM announcement'. This is merely an audience measurement and in no way constitutes an offer of any kind. But, you will be helping us with the programming of this station. Remember, if you heard this announcement, please write a letter to WERE, Cleveland 15, Ohio. Thank you for your cooperation."

Maybe it was the lack of FM tuners or, more likely, a lack of interest, but the response was underwhelming. WERE, like most stations, just kept simulcasting until the FCC required separate FM programming starting in 1968. Then, it wasn't too long before broadcasters would discover that the sound of cash registers came across so much clearer out of stereo speakers.

Wayne Mack and WDOK-AM were a pair until December 1965.

In the 1950s, *Time* magazine named WERE's Bill Randle the most important radio personality in the country. Randle turned down an offer to manage Elvis Presley because he didn't have the time. *Cleveland Press Collection, Cleveland State University Archives*

That's when the AM became WIXY 1260, and Mack was banished to program "the lands of the Western Reserve" on the FM side. Mack made money and ratings for the owners on the FM, but his fans missed him on the more popular AM band. WIXY got huge ratings and was a giant in the industry until FM started to eat up all the AM outlets. In 1976 the station took the call letters WMGC and, in a very conservative Northeast Ohio, caused an uproar with billboards stating, "Get Your Rock Soft." Three years later, it became WBBG, tried and failed with a talk format, and after a lot of tweaking switched to the same music Mack used to play!

Some said WBBG stood for "Big Band Grandstand," and it did pretty well until the format switched over to WRMR, the old WJW, in 1987. A lot of the old war horses of Cleveland radio (and that is said with the greatest respect) found a new home with an old audience. It was like a time machine! Carl Reese, Ronnie Barrett, the great Bill Randle . . . and the return of Wayne Mack!

Mack hit the ground running, too. The Palace Ballroom was back on the air, and it had plenty of star power, too. One night in 1993 Mack promised a huge live show with Barbra Streisand singing with Harry James and his orchestra. What made the night even more remarkable was that James had died ten years earlier. No wonder Mack said there were "twenty-six charter buses already parked together and traffic was bumper to bumper on Morningside Drive all the way to Indian Ridge." WRMR wisely had a disclaimer before every broadcast saying, "Ladies and gentlemen. The following program is pure fantasy, and is not to be confused with any actual place or event. The setting is fictional, and the music is on records and tapes and is intended solely for the entertainment of our listening audience." The station still took calls asking for directions from listeners who probably shouldn't have still been driving.

Mack hung on for a good long time, but his health caught up with him. He eventually did what most of his audience had done long before and retired. Pardon the cliché, but Wayne Mack went to the big ballroom in the sky on October 15, 2000.

Let's go back to Bill Randle.

Randle's life took a few twists and turns after he left WERE, teaching college classes, picking up a few degrees, and getting his license to practice law. But he kept his toe in the radio pool and, as always, did what he wanted. Program directors knew better than to try to tell Randle what to do. At WRMR he played *NSync along with the "Music of Your Life," and was one of the first jocks to play 13-year-old LeeAnn Rimes, saying she was going to be a huge star. His audience stayed with him, too.

He also didn't care what he said to whom or where. One Sunday night there was a broadcasters' event at a hotel in Akron, and Randle was being honored along with Mike Douglas and some other big names. It wasn't formal, but most people were in suits and ties—except Randle: open collar, shirt sleeves rolled up to his elbows, and you could tell Randle was waiting for someone to say something. The night was going long, and it was finally time for Randle to speak. This was some speech!

Randle told everyone that awards ceremonies and the people behind them are stupid and this was a good example. It was going way too long, and he didn't need a cheap plaque or a dinner to show he had done something significant. He already knew it, and so did anyone else with a brain. Then he talked about the way radio had degenerated and called one of the current afternoon hosts a "functional illiterate." He ended his speech—if you call it that—by saying, "One more thing. I don't believe in God either. What do you think about that?" He left the podium, walked through a crowd of people with their mouths wide open and went through the door to his car.

Eventually, Bill Randle became ill, and as his condition worsened he would "voice track" his show. That's just a way of digitally recording segments and inserting them between songs. It usually takes 20 minutes to half an hour to lay down the tracks for a four-hour show, but Randle was so weak he would have to rest and it could take him the entire four hours. But as long as there was a place for him to broadcast, he was going to be there.

But WRMR had its own health issues. A loyal audience, good ratings, but let's face facts—who's going to buy ad time on a station that caters to people on fixed incomes? People and formats get old, and the comment was that every funeral procession was another 'RMR listener who wouldn't be replaced. The staff joked that the station's demos were "55 to dead." The decision came down to pull the plug on the format, and the final day would be Friday, July 9, 2004. Morning drive ended at 10 a.m. that day, and Ted Alexander came on to do the top-of-the-hour news break. You could tell by his voice that something was wrong. He was shaken and choking back tears, and it wasn't because of the end of WRMR.

"I was afraid this day would come, and as Jackie Gerber, our morning host on WCLV says, almost cosmic. WRMR is sad to announce that Cleveland radio personality Bill Randle passed away this morning." He went on after a pause, "That's pretty tough to say. He'd been ill for an extended time. He was born in Detroit, Michigan in 1924. At the age of 16 he started his journey into broadcasting. He introduced big bands on live radio. He ran a nightclub. He was a concert organizer. He held a doctorate in history. Was a practicing lawyer. *Time* magazine once called him 'the number one disc jockey in America.' Bill Randle."

You can tell he was struggling, but Alexander soldiered on. "He was the host of the number one radio show in Cleveland on WERE during the week, and the number one radio show in New York City on WCBS on the weekends. People in the industry knew that if he said something was the next big thing, they could take it to the bank. He's been writing books and he's been educating himself for years and years. Had many degrees. At one time in his night club he hired a bouncer up in Detroit, Michigan, called 'Detroit Red'. Later he was known as Malcolm X. Bill, of course, was credited with discovering Elvis Presley, and also Johnnie Ray. Bill also introduced Elvis the first time he was on national TV. Elvis's career was launched with Bill playing his records first in Cleveland and then in New York.

"Some of the things that Bill Randle did, he made the Mormon Tabernacle Choir's recording of 'The Battle Hymn of the Republic' a national hit by simply editing the playing time so it would fit into radio station music schedules for short Top 40 records of the day. After his time on WERE Bill Randle was heard on WBBG 1260 and WRMR 850, sometimes on the air seven days a week. In July 2001, when WRMR 850 switched formats to sports and talk and became WKNR, the standards format came over here." (Editor's note: The format and call letters went to 1420 AM, the old WHK.)

He went on to say, "Bill retired for a while to concentrate on his law practice, but he couldn't stay away from the microphone. So, in July of 2002, Bill was invited back to WRMR and the Cleveland airwaves, first reviving his Juke Box Saturday Night show from 7 to 10, and the Big Show on Sundays." Alexander started to break down, and ended with "God rest your soul, Bill."

The remaining hours of WRMR turned into a tribute to one of the most important jocks ever. The day the music died, revisited. Bill Randle had a huge ego, but he had sure earned it. He didn't hold anything back. You can't help but think that Randle was ushered through the pearly gates and told, "The boss wants to see you right away." And as he stood before the big throne, the angels heard Randle say to the man in charge, "By the way, I don't believe in you!"

That was Bill Randle!

Power to the People!

Tales from the Technical Side

RADIO CAN BE HIGHLY organized or very loose and free-wheeling. It depends on the formats and personalities. Sales and ratings can go up or down, but none of that matters if it falls short on the technical end. Technical people are usually the last to be congratulated and the first to be criticized, so the pressure is on from the day you sign on board. Frank Foti can tell you firsthand.

"I started working at Malrite and WMMS around Thanksgiving of 1978," Foti recalls. "They moved to the Statler Office Tower, one of the stations, on Valentines Day 1977 and the other station one week later. There was still a lot to get done when I got there a few months later. One of the problems was that Flash Ferenc used to do a public affairs program called 'We the People,' and John Gorman said they received some listener mail that said whenever they ran the segment—it was only a five-minute thing every day—that on some radios you couldn't hear it! Huh? After thinking about it, it was on clock radios that were mono, and someone screwed up on one of the tape machines in the back of the production room to where the audio was out of phase. They'd wired the input and the output out of phase so when you played it out of that tape machine in the production studio it was fine, but when it played out of the machines in the air studio the out-of-phase stuff cancelled out in mono. I remember Somich putting me on that and I spent an entire weekend at the radio station trying to figure it out. The point is, there were a bunch of little crazy things that were poorly done and rushed. It was probably a couple of years after they were at the Statler that we got everything settled down in regard to 'HK and 'MMS."

Welcome to major market radio!

Foti will also tell you it's exactly why you went into radio.

"I was a kid who grew up in Wickliffe, Ohio, and WMMS was the hallowed halls! Being a kid who grew up on rock and roll, and at the same time knowing radio and WHK was no small thing either, I though, *Wow, man! These are all the people that I listened to! I'm working with them!* It took me a couple of months to get over that. Jeff and Flash, Matt the Cat, that kind of thing.

"Also, WHK has two of the highest-paid radio personalities in America, Gary Dee in the morning and Don Imus in the afternoon. You heard a lot about Gary getting in trouble with Liz Richards, and stories about Imus at NBC. I was in my early twenties, and remember thinking the thing that really struck me so much was how down to earth everybody was. Off the air, Gary was always kind of low key. He had a big interest in model remote controlled airplanes. Every once in a while, he would walk into the engineering shop with some little thing from his controller and he'd say, 'They're telling me it's going to cost a hundred dollars to get this piece soldered!' 'Gary, Gary. Go get a cup of coffee.' He'd come back and I'd fix it for him. Imus, too."

Everyone knew everyone else on a very personal level. Sometimes that could be very hard.

Foti recalls the death of the Yankees' Thurman Munson. "I was out at the transmitter site, and we had to switch something because of a thunderstorm that affected the actual transmitter. My nature was always to call the studio and let the guys know that if they hear the station go down there's nothing wrong. Imus picked up the hotline, and he sounded like death warmed over. He said, 'Hey man. My buddy died.' The thing about Imus is that you never knew if he was jerking your chain, because he was as sarcastic off the air as he was on. He said, 'Thurman Munson was a friend of mine,' and on and on and he was talking to me while Marv Boone was doing the news, and in the background I could hear Marv saying, 'We're in shock right now because we just got a report that Thurman Munson's plane crashed at the Canton Airport.' That stuck with me because I remember how real that was and how quickly life can go away, and how moved Don Imus was."

There was plenty of room for some very creative chicanery, especially on the WMMS side. "I remember Jeff [Kinzbach] and I taping M-100 fireworks to balsa planes. We would light them and toss them out the back window of the engineering shop. One time, we figured it would fly over the parking lot and from twelve stories up we would watch it explode. What we didn't realize was that it would circle back and hover along the side of the building. We heard it explode, and that was when the Statler was also a hotel as well as an office building. It took out a window!" Thankfully, these were the days before Trip Adviser.

Foti says you got to see other sides of their personalities as well.

"I remember Kid Leo's passion. Leo knew the staff so well. I was walking down the hall and he said, 'For someone who likes The Who and the Kinks as much as you do, you might want to go to the Agora tonight. There's this band that I think you're going to like. They're called the Pretenders.' He knew me that well."

And it wasn't always about the music.

"One thing about Betty Korvan," Foti says. "She's a huge baseball fan. Massive baseball fan. One day we were at a jock meeting, and the Boston Red Sox were in town with this relief pitcher named Bill Lee. This guy was out there! It later came out that the guy used to trip on LSD. Betty was kind of in a funk because she really wanted to go and see the Red Sox with Bill Lee on the mound. 'Hey Betty, I'll go to the game with you.' We met up at the station at East 12th and Chester around dinner time and walked over to the old Cleveland Stadium on West Sixth, watched the game through maybe the sixth or seventh inning, and we walked back to the station because she had to do her show.

"Here you have this well known rock and roll disc jockey with great stories about all these rock stars. We used to argue like crazy about who was a better guitar player, The Who's Pete Townshend or Jimmy Page with Led Zeppelin. Betty was just as passionate about Led Zeppelin and the Stones. All of them at WMMS and

WHK, their passion for what went on the radio came through every time they switched on the mic. I was just the kid from Wickliffe who got to be a part of it."

Sometimes the engineering department could get very creative, often out of necessity.

"I still have the stereo amplifier that I built in high school, and it still runs," Foti says. "In the early days, we had some stuff at WMMS that was from Heathkit [the electronics parts company popular with hobbyists] because there were certain pieces of test gear that we wanted but corporate wasn't going to give us the approval for it, but if there was a variant of it that Heathkit made we used that for pennies on the dollar."

Some folks turned ideas into reality. "Steve Church's first interface system, Telos 10, he had already had it as a product when he came to work at 'MMS, but within WMMS and WHK there were hand-built things that had to do with audio consoles and processing. We also came up with a pretty creative way to quickly switch the transmitters for AM and FM and also to notify us if there was a problem. We were just resourceful with a lot of things. Not only did we build it but over at East 14th and Prospect was the old electronics surplus store. There was a lot of stuff that came out of that surplus store that ended up on those radio stations."

So, from his perspective, with all the pressure in every department, what made Malrite run like a machine?

"At that time they were in the zone," Foti says. "Milt basically had within himself and the people he found to be in his company an esprit de corps. People that were driven, that became overachievers because they were passionate and played to win because they wouldn't play to lose. When you look at the diverse backgrounds of all these individuals—I mean you had folks in management like John Gorman and all the way to very successful people in sales on 'MMS and WHK. I have to give credit to Mr. Maltz. Somehow it filtered down from him to the people he hired and those that they hired that they had to be the best. They also found a way to be the best even if they didn't have the money to be the best.

"Back in the days when we would get the ratings period underway, John Gorman would put out the memos that said, 'Kill! Maim! Destroy!' It was John's way of getting us motivated. You'd walk into the air studio, and the station's art director David Helton would have a poster board sketch in Sharpie of the Buzzard pulling on a rope with a pulley. On the other end of the pulley it was attached to the gonads of 'the Chimp,' the program director at M105 [WMMM-FM], our main competitor. I loved that!

"For as crazy as it might have appeared, as crazy as John Gorman could get, I loved that attitude that we had to get out there and kill. Or Kid Leo, his passion! I fed off it."

The following story wasn't on the technical side, but it illustrates the creativity on every level at WMMS. During the Who's so-called "Farewell Tour" in December 1982 (the first of several such tours), the band, which loved Cleveland, booked two shows at the Richfield Coliseum. These were expected to be the final shows in the United States. (Toronto would host the swan song.) WMMS asked what it would take to get their call letters on every ticket. It could be done, they were told, but the station would have to buy every seat—all 40,000 of them—and there were rumors that the station paid an extra dollar per ticket to have "WMMS Presents The Who" printed on top. What's the return on this? Plenty, and some things that no one anticipated.

WGCL and other stations were assured they would be able to buy tickets for giveaways. It wasn't likely they would be very good seats, but they were free for a show that sold out immediately. G98 was a primary target of the Buzzards. How was WGCL, or any station for that matter, expected to give away tickets with WMMS popping out? It was bad enough that WMMS was often heard over the public address system before the opening act. Someone at G98 took a black magic marker and crossed out the "WMMS Presents" line. This, it turned out, was not a good idea.

How many tickets did WGCL give out? Maybe a hundred per

show? Keep this in mind. There were no tickets available. You either had one or you didn't have a seat.

Early in the evening of the first show, the phones started ringing at WGCL, and these callers weren't requesting songs! Ushers at the Coliseum were refusing entry because the tickets had been altered! One call after another after another.

The next morning, there was an angry crowd outside the studios at East 15th and Chester, and if someone had been nearby selling pitchforks and torches they would have made a bundle. Promises were made for restitution, but that didn't really appease anyone. And the second show was coming up that night. WGCL became a bunker through no one's fault but its own. Incidents like that that made for great memories at WMMS.

Foti was fortunate to have worked for Malrite in Cleveland and also at Z100 in New York, with similar results.

"Steve Church and I used to say this all the time," Foti says. "Who would have thought that two lower-middle-class, blue-collar kids from the Midwest—rugrats in radio—that we would get the opportunity to see the world and in that journey to be a part of something like WMMS, WHK, and even Z100.

"I'm ecstatic that the Cleveland Cavaliers became champions [in 2016], but I got to do it two-three times."

Air Pirates

Illegal Radio Stations vs. the Feds

MAPLE HEIGHTS IS LIKE a lot of middle-class suburbs around the Greater Cleveland area. Southgate Shopping Center was right down the street, and it was a short hop to downtown Cleveland. It also had a very professionally run radio station, WMHR, "Maple Heights Radio, 16-0-0 on your radio!" The staff called it "the happiest station in town." One problem, though.

It never had a license.

WMHR was a pirate radio station. They weren't alone. There were pirate stations all over Northeast Ohio, and the Federal Communications Commission was not happy. Here's the way it way it usually worked: Some folks would get a surplus army transmitter or build one themselves, set up a turntable and a microphone, and they were on the air. But as soon as you flipped that on-air switch, you dipped your toe in some dangerous waters.

This wasn't really anything new. A couple of years before, there was another station up in Mayfield Heights. You could find WMFH on your dial at 540 AM, and the staff ranged in age from 10 to 15 years old. They were on the air for a few hours on weeknights in the summer from 5:30 to 9 p.m., and 7 to 9 during the school year—after they did their home work. They aired pop music, weather, and news that they got from the *Cleveland Press*. That might have been what brought down the hammer. In July 1960, the *Press* ran a story about the kids, including their photos, ages, and home addresses. (They always included home addresses for everyone they ran a story about, and those were the days when everyone had a listed phone number.) The bottom line is the newspaper

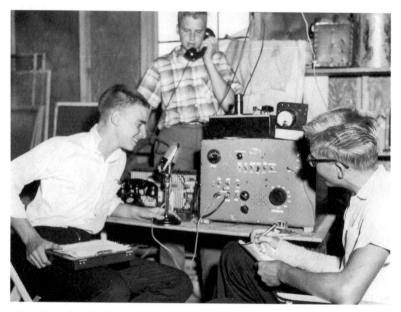

Not all amateur stations operated outside the law. Early amateur operators in Parma ran a sophisticated operation out of a garage. Trouble came when you started cutting into the commercial signals. *Cleveland Press Collection, Cleveland State University Archives*

showed seven kids violating federal law—and told the feds exactly where to find them.

Turns out, the kids were encouraged to start their station by a neighbor who was a radio professional.

Arnie Rosenberg was a legend in the Cleveland radio community. At the time he was an engineer at WERE, and one of the old vets who was a "go-to guy" if you had a problem. Engineers at other stations would call him for advice, and he was glad to help out. He lived next door to the kid who started the station in his basement, and offered to let him use some of his equipment and an old radio transmitter he had at his house to get the station on the air. "I used to have my own station," Rosenberg said, "but since I got married I don't have the time anymore."

They actually had an AM transmitter, but it was too big to haul so they just ran a line next door, and the power lines were the

The transmitter antenna for WKOS rose high above a
garage on Memphis Avenue. The young jocks had shifts,
plenty of records, and an experienced engineer. Very professional . . . and very illegal. *Cleveland Press Collection, Cleveland
State University Archives*

antenna. It also operated on a special carrier current, meaning your
antennas had to be aimed at telephone lines to pick up the signal.

One of the young jocks, Ray Glasser, remembers, "Arnie wanted
us to put the station on the air. He built the mixing board, set
up two turntables to play LPs and 45 records, and hooked up the
mike. He even brought overstock records from WERE. We all had
half-hour shifts. Kept program logs, too. Very professional."

Arnie Rosenberg held a federally issued, first-class operator's
license. He had to know the risks. These kids had to be awfully
special to him!

The station was only on the air from April to August 1960. As

Station WMHR even fooled Maple Heights city officials, who gave the pirates funding to publicize the city's anniversary celebration. The station stopped celebrating when agents from the Federal Communications Commission swooped in.
Cleveland Press Collection, Cleveland State University Archives

Glasser tells it, "We had to worry about school first. We didn't have time for both radio and homework."

Most of the pirate stations like WMFH had a very small reach, usually just a mile or two. WHAT wasn't heard much outside of Bob's Trailer City on Rockside Road in Bedford Heights, and that's probably very fortunate. The Bedford Heights police station was right around the corner, and the station's sole disc jockey, Tim Buday, would often do lengthy commentaries on his personal pub crawls.

How about WIKD 1390 or WBDJ 1460? KAOS may have been in the 900 or 1000 kilohertz range, with pirate stations all around the Southeast suburbs in mid to late 1960s. It was almost always a Top 40 format, and WMHR was king of them all.

They used the telephone company test lines to take requests

so a phone number couldn't be traced. As one of the pirate jocks (who will remain anonymous), recalls, "These were also known as click lines, and each exchange had a pair of numbers that would be matched up, say 555-9883 and 555-9884. Not sure if those were the actual last four numbers used because it was so long ago. The jock would be already listening on 9883 for a caller to request a tune when he or she would call 9884. There would be brief drop-out in the conversation every few seconds, but you wouldn't lose the connection. I think that was the 'click' the click lines were named for. Fun times."

The stations would last a couple months then move to a new location so the FCC wouldn't catch on. They would start up again with new call letters and frequency in hopes they wouldn't get shut down.

WMHR was the brainchild of Don Boehnlein, who would use the name Don Allen when he landed a gig at WXEN. It was amazing that he was able to keep that job at WXEN because, even though he had a driver's license, he would hitchhike to work. To his credit, he rarely missed a day or even came in late.

Memories are fuzzy, but one of the folks who associated with Boehnlein remembers him stringing a wire up a phone line for a transmitting antenna. There's another story that he used the gutters of his house. There are sketchy memories about the transmitter, too. It could have been a modified army surplus transmitter, or even a Heathkit project. However he did it, he got the station on the air. It was only five watts, but WMHR covered a pretty good-sized area. Reports came in from East 128th and Broadway in Cleveland, Shaker Heights, and other suburbs on the southeast side of the city.

The jocks may have sounded a little raw, but overall the station sounded very professional. Even Maple Heights city officials thought the station was legit. During the city's fiftieth anniversary in 1965, the city paid WMHR $500 to promote the celebration as its "official radio station." 'MHR used some of the money to print bumper stickers promoting an illegal facility!

Boehnlein was pretty bold. He not only had a pirate station on the air, but he even sold advertising. Not only that, he took the show on the road and did remotes! An ice cream parlor and the Oriental Terrace restaurant at Southgate opened their doors to WMHR. And then there was the Chanel High School Firebird Festival. It was just down the road in Bedford, and the school put on a carnival to raise funds for its football team. They set up on the field and WMHR was there for a live broadcast. Ernie Kellerman was a Chanel grad and was a defensive back for the Cleveland Browns. He was also a pretty good quarterback and showed it at the Firebird Festival, easily tossing footballs through a target down the field. Boehnlein asked him to do a quick on-air interview, and Kellerman was happy to do so. How could he know this was a bootleg operation? No one did. There was a story that Kellerman accepted an invitation to drop by the studios, and was surprised to see it was a house in a residential neighborhood. There were reports that Kellerman went on the air there as well, though there's no real proof. Memories fade, and efforts to contact Kellerman to ask him about that story hit a wall.

Bold took on a different meaning with an incident near a transmitter site. Boehnlein was testing out the equipment at a friend's house and glanced out the window to see a car with a suspicious antenna array slowly driving by. The driver looked pretty young, and Boehnlein chased after him to see why he was driving around. Those were days before convenience stores like Open Pantrys and 7-Elevens. You saw a Lawson's store here and there, but most neighborhoods had the "mom and pop" grocery and delis and that's where Boehnlein caught up with the guy at a local deli. Turned out he was just a radio ham operator who was tracking the signal with "triangulation" to see where it was coming from. Now, keep in mind that WMHR advertised its location on the dial, gave its studio address, the times it was on the air and, at one point before the click line, even used a home phone number. It would seem the clock was ticking.

Time eventually ran out for WMHR, and there was a knock on

Boehnlein's door. Memories are little sketchy, but a couple of the jocks, who are still afraid of the feds and want to stay anonymous, gave these accounts. They say three men entered and one went directly to Boehnlein's frightened parents to say they were shutting down the illegal operation and there would be a fine of $1,500 if it ever went back on the air. That's $1,500 in 1960s dollars.

One of the feds was Ed Atems, the dreaded FCC agent from Detroit whom pirate stations openly mocked and dedicated songs to. He didn't find that amusing, but he did enjoy shutting down bootleg stations. One jock said Atems went on the air, declared the station an illegal operation and officially signed it off with a time check. One source recalls that the two men opened a brief case and, using electronic hook-ups, burned out the equipment and broke tubes; another remembers them seizing the gear. However it happened, WMHR was now broadcast history.

Several folks who passed through Boehnlein's "studios" went on to professional careers in radio and TV. One of them was Carl Monday, who did some air time on WMHR. He was only a teenager, but the radio bug bit Carl and he decided to start a station of his own. He set up shop in the basement of his home on Donovan Avenue in Garfield Heights. It wasn't long before WNTR radio was on the air. It's slogan was "Winter all Summer," but it didn't even last that long. After a few weeks, Carl faced an opponent that was far more intimidating and worked faster than the FCC. His station in the basement was affecting TV and radio reception in the floors above. His mom marched downstairs and pulled the cords. Like the season, WNTR faded into memory.

Mama, Don't Let Your Cowboys Grow Up to Be Deejays

Doc Lemon, Cleveland's Man in Black

MALRITE COMMUNICATIONS KNEW HOW to hire personalities. The WMMS staff was full of unique air talent, but there was no shortage of wild and wacky on its AM sister station, WHK, especially during the country format era. We've had a look at Gary Dee and Joe Finan in other chapters of this book, but there were plenty more characters. Don Imus came back to do afternoons and brought his brother Fred along to do fill-in air shifts and production. There was "Wild Bill" Wilkins who would drink at the Statler Office Tower's Terrace Club to get ready for his show several hours later.

Then there was Doc Lemon, the overnight guy, a hard-drinking cowboy whose reputation went well beyond his air work.

Betty Korvan worked across the hall at WMMS, and she remembered Doc as a master at making at chili. John Webster, who was at WHK and remembered Doc well, wrote in his memoirs that when Lemon was at WHK in the 1970s and early 1980s, folks guessed his age to be in the early sixties. He put a lot into those years, too, and mostly out of a bottle. Doc would get off the air at 6, crack a beer open in his truck, and visit friends at other stations. He'd often stop to visit Jim Hale at WERE, where he could be recognized on the security camera with his black hat pulled down low and sipping one of his "eye openers."

About that hat.

Doc loved the country lifestyle of that time, which was a far cry from the sophisticated artists and fashions of today. Webster

Cleveland's favorite cowboy, Doc Lemon, loved country
music, chili, women, and beer . . . and sometimes a quick
nap on the air. *George Shuba*

remembers Doc as an old-time cowboy. "He dressed totally in
black, including a ten-gallon hat, string tie, and cowboy boots. He
drove a pick-up truck that was stenciled in several places: DOC
LEMON, COUNTRY MUSIC, MIDNIGHT TO SIX, WHK, 1420.
The passenger seat was replaced with what appeared to be a bench
but was really a beer cooler that he filled to the brim every day."

As Webster recalls, the fans loved him, and he drew crowds at
his appearances at the Cuyahoga County Fair, country music bars,
and at nearly every concert featuring big-time country music stars.
His stories usually started the same way: "Tossed back a few backstage with (fill-in the artist's name.)" He knocked them back with

Willie Nelson, Waylon Jennings, you name them. Doc knew them all and knew what they drank.

Webster quotes one-time station manager Gil Rosenwald as saying, "Most of the time his heavy drinking didn't affect his performance. When it gets out of hand, we warn him and he always seems to settle down for a while afterwards. Besides, we absolutely forbid alcohol in the studio." Like that was going to stop the Doc! He carried an old boom box radio where ever he went—at least it looked like a boom box. The electronics had been removed to make just enough room for a fifth of whiskey.

Who's at a radio station overnight? Of course, the jocks and maybe a newsperson, but that's pretty much it. Doc would crack open beers, drink during his show, and clean up the "dead soldiers" so there was no evidence. It was a good plan when it worked, but one day the Shaker Heights Police Department started getting calls about problems at WHK. They didn't have jurisdiction, but they tuned in a radio and it was pretty obvious something wasn't right. They got a number for WHK's program director and told him, "There's something wrong at your radio station. All we hear is a funny noise."

At three in the morning, the program director switched on his bedside radio and there it was, the unmistakable sound of a record clicking in the final groove! Calls to the station hot line went unanswered, and so did calls to the Statler's night clerk. Only one thing to do. The PD threw on some clothes, jumped on his motorcycle and headed downtown.

This visit gave the term dysfunctional a whole new meaning. The Statler's night clerk refused to wake up to operate the manual elevators, so what were the options? How about twelve flights of stairs? He finally made it to the station and mustered up enough energy to burst into the WHK studio. The stench of booze was overwhelming, and there was Doc, snoring like a buzzsaw with his head perched on the control console. The record was skipping merrily away.

Still out of breath, the PD yelled, "Doc! Doc! You alright?" That was enough to get Doc to raise his head and mumble into the microphone, "Radio fourteen. WHK." Then he switched off the mic, his head crashed back onto the console and went back to sawing wood. They wheeled him and his phony radio out of the studio, but get this—he kept his job! He wasn't even suspended! Rosenwald decided not to penalize him, because, "Doc brings a lot of advertising business to the station, so we should be willing to put up with his idiosyncrasies."

Doc showed up for his show the following night as if nothing had happened and said he didn't remember anything. He kept his gig with WHK until 1984, when the station changed to a (short-lived) format of rock and roll oldies called 14K. Doc was found dead a few months later in his camping trailer parked at Chippewa Lake, still dressed in black. His big Stetson hat was crushed under his head. The cause was no surprise. "Booze killed him," the coroner said. "His liver swelled up to the size of a bushel basket and just quit working."

A sad end for a radio cowboy. Fade to black.

At Your Service

Public Service Programming and the
Sunday Morning Graveyard

MENTION THE WORDS PUBLIC service to radio programmers and they'll usually yawn in your face. But the term public service can be defined in many different ways, and radio stations could be very creative. Just for the record, when a station reapplies for its license renewal every few years it has to prove that it has provided a service to its listeners. Every three months, it files a report with the FCC with the special interest programs, public service announcements and even station events that fit that description. For example, if a station was part of a food or clothing drive, it provided some sort of verification and put that in the file. But you still have to put words "in the air."

Most stations don't want to risk ratings with boring programming, so they'll push those shows into the "Sunday morning graveyard." Those are the early hours when very few people are awake and even fewer are listening to the radio. So what do you put on? No one puts a lot of thought into that, as long as it fits the FCC guidelines. You have to provide so many hours every week, so a lot of stations will record the Cleveland City Club's live broadcast on Friday and re-air it that weekend. That show usually has some pretty compelling guests and is syndicated across the country, even if the topics are often local to Northeast Ohio. If you're affiliated with a network, the chances are you'll carry one of their medical shows. News used to qualify, but once newsrooms started turning a profit, the FCC looked at news differently.

So how do you fill out the rest of the time?

The early FM rockers really took the lead on this. Martin Perlich's *Perlich Project* was on WCLV. That's right, the station would leave classical programming and go to a free form show after midnight. But that didn't mean it was exclusively rock. There was folk, classical, jazz, and anything that sounded good together. Perlich also invited guests to discuss issues between the songs, and that ranged from high school dress codes and local politics to race relations and the Kent State shootings. Perlich spoke just as passionately about the life and legacy of composer George Szell as he did about Jimi Hendrix when news broke that they died.

Shauna Zurbrugg and Jeff Gelb at WNCR had *People's Want Ads*. You'd call in with some type of product or service and what you wanted in return. It could be a pair of pants you grew out of, someone to share a ride to Chicago, an old musical instrument to trade, the list went on. They'd also put your phone number on the air, but there were few if any complaints. It was a different time.

Around that same time at WMMS you had shows that ran prime time on Saturdays and Sundays covering gay rights, women's liberation, student rights, and even a prisoner call-in show. In the Vietnam years, the station carried the military draft lottery live and offered numbers for counseling if you had a low number. There were also recorded vignettes like *We the People* and *Jabberwocky* that looked at a wide range of issues and ran during the day. *Jabberwocky* later became a half-hour interview show that ran early morning on Sunday along with NBC's *Source Report*, a news program that profiled everything from international trade to Bettie Page, the lingerie model from the 1950s.

Then there were certain lifestyle issues.

In the early 1970s, the Cleveland police joined with WMMS to offer free testing of listeners' weed to check for paraquat, a defoliant sprayed on marijuana fields that could seriously affect you if it was ingested. Here's the problem: You were supposed to send a sample to the main police station, include a number sequence to identify your stuff, wait a few days, and call a phone number to hear the results—too many numbers for people who had probably "done a number." Plus, some listeners just didn't listen. They would include return addresses, some dropped it off in person, would send pills or even drop off a whole ounce and ask the cops to return what they didn't use. That promotion came to a quick end when listeners started sending the stuff to the radio station. The postal service and radio stations are all overseen by the feds, and WMMS pulled the plug to protect their license.

Drug references were common on early FM rock. It was part of the counterculture, and Murray Saul was right in the thick of it. He also made no secret of the fact that he liked ganja and talked about it openly in his Friday "Get Downs." So how was that a public service? This may be stretching it a bit, but when Murray talked about the red and gold leaves on the street he was referring to the Panama and Acapulco varieties, and not the stuff you raked off the lawn. Then there was a special mention every day in the afternoon news.

WMMS always had a strong news presence, with reports through the morning, at noon, and in afternoon drive. The afternoon news person would get a call from a local stock broker with the closing Dow Jones average. If you didn't have it in the newscast the switchboard, request lines and newsroom phones would light up all at once, and you made sure you got it on as soon as possible. A lot of times you would hear the sounds of factories or taverns in the background. These weren't people with stock portfolios. In the days before a daily state lottery, the Dow average was the daily number. The station just gave them the daily stock closing. They didn't tell them what to do with it. The rest was up to you and your bookie. It's unlikely any of this was included in the public service filing.

One of the most memorable examples of a public service took a lot of guts and some very brave people to get it on the air.

At one time Glenville was a great area, but its best years were long behind it. The neighborhood that gave the world the creators of Superman, *Inherit the Wind,* and *How to Succeed in Business Without Even Trying* was now mainly working poor. Urban flight to the suburbs brought a lot of African-American families to Glen-

The disc jockeys at WABQ helped redefine public service on the radio. It took a riot to prove their point. *Cleveland Press Collection, Cleveland State University Archives*

ville, and they wanted to succeed, too. Inner-city Cleveland was a tough place, and the 1960s were a tough time. There was a lot of racial tension there and across the country, and people were frustrated. They talked about it on the streets, and in the pages of the *Call and Post* newspaper. It got a lot of attention on the radio, too.

WABQ was a daytime AM station, which meant it went on at daybreak and off at dusk so it wouldn't interfere with signals from other stations. The broadcast day was pretty much determined by the seasons. It was only a thousand watts, but "Tiger Radio" had a very loyal following with the urban audience and put up a good fight against WJMO with a similar format. It was in for a different fight when the riots broke out on July 23, 1968.

Glenville was like a lot of working poor urban neighborhoods across America. Jobs were few, and racial bias kept a lot of people from getting ahead. Gunshots were commonly heard in these type of neighborhoods, especially during the hot summer months, but something happened that July day that quickly spun out of control.

A confrontation in Glenville between Cleveland Police and a group called the Black Nationalists of New Libya left seven people dead, including three policemen, and fifteen others wounded. It quickly escalated into a devastating, full-scale riot. Neighborhood community leaders tried to ease the tensions, but that failed and Mayor Carl Stokes called in the Ohio National Guard. With heavy gunfire, it was not safe for anyone to be on the street. It was not much better indoors, but at least it gave you a chance. Someone had to get the word out, someone the neighbors there trusted, and that job fell on the staff of WABQ.

The call letters stood for "We Are Better Qualified" and they rose to the task that night. Early in the evening, when the first reports started coming in, the news staff and jocks knew they had a big job ahead. The jock on the air was Michael "The Lover" Payne, a longtime favorite and one of the most trusted voices in Cleveland's black community. You knew something was wrong when he played the station's emergency broadcast warning that started with, "Listen for this sound," with a sharp beeping noise. It warned that a message of vital importance would be forthcoming from the Cleveland Police. It might even tell off-duty police to report to their station houses immediately, but whatever it signaled, it wasn't good. This was just a warning before Payne took over. Then, the nightly jingle introducing the man who "filled the hole in your soul, who was so down he had every chick in town and the plan that had cats eating out of his hand."

Payne was now in the driver's seat, and launched right into a Sam and Dave tune while reports started to trickle in from the street. In mid-summer the station could stay on until around 9 p.m. but that didn't affect the situation that was tearing Glenville apart. Payne tried to act upbeat, but the situation was impossible to ignore and he started putting calls on the air from black and white listeners. Soon he was joined by staffers John Jay and Curtis Shaw with news updates from Van Lane. The mission was to ease the tension, though some of the calls were clearly antagonistic.

The air staff opened the lines and constantly reassured the audi-

Michael "The Lover" Payne calmed the nerves of his WABQ audience during one of the most tense periods in Cleveland history. *Cleveland Press Collection, Cleveland State University Archives*

ence that every effort was being made to maintain order. All this time, the sun was starting to set and decisions had to be made. They had to sign off at sunset—or did they? The reason many stations sign off is so their signals don't interfere with those from other cities that traveled farther at night. Did those cities have to deal with riots? We're staying on the air!

There was an occasional song so the staffers could determine their next step, but they stayed the course and remained on the air all night—in clear violation of the terms of their license and the Federal Communications Commission. After that first night, the station saw enough outside media to go back to its original sign-off time, but that's when it got a little complicated. Someone complained to the FCC that WABQ had remained on the air, and that could affect the station's license renewal.

Lawyers debated for months that turned into years, but finally WABQ's legal team laid it out to the FCC. WABQ had been granted a license to serve the public. What greater public service could they have performed than helping to save lives and keeping people in their homes near a radio? The FCC thought they made a very compelling argument and finally put the matter to rest without any further action.

Short Circuits

WE HAVE SOME STORIES that bear repeating. They're part of a greater story, but are being told separately because they're so unusual.

Maybe it was numerology, or even astrology, but four Cleveland newsmen were born within six days of each other in mid-1953. We won't mention the exact dates for sake of privacy. First there was Tom Bell who started at WJW, would go on to CKLW and eventually a management position in TV. Bob Becker is next. He worked at WNCR, WERE, WGAR and WWWE/WTAM, as well as in TV at WKYC and as host of the weekly Ohio Lottery program on WEWS. Yours truly, Mike Olszewski, was born on the same exact day. I also went to school with Tom Bell at Bedford High, and did time at WERE, WMMS, and WZJM. Plus, like Tom and Bob, I worked in TV as well. Finally, Ed Ferenc came into the world at the same time and cut his teeth at WMMS before heading to WWWE/WTAM.

And now a look at radio folks and cars. Milt Fullerton had a long resume by the time he landed at WERE in the early 1980s. He'd been a network foreign correspondent and did some impressive work in Europe at a number of historic events. Everyone loved Milt. He looked and acted like Shakespeare's Falstaff, a big, imposing figure who loved socializing with everyone at just about every station. When he was news director, his meetings with staff would often turn into small dinner parties at the Park Center restaurants, with plenty of booze and lots of laughs. People from other stations would invite him to parties, and because he lived a couple of blocks from the station and didn't have a car, he would borrow one of the WERE news cars. He'd take the car, bring it back in a few hours, and walk home. Most of the time.

Milt was invited to a party in Akron, and that's a good hour from downtown Cleveland if you're doing the speed limit. Let me also point out that the WERE news cars were borderline death traps. Reporters would take them out, and if something was wrong they might or might not report it, and there was even less chance the care would be repaired. If the engine started, you took a shot. That didn't bother Milt. One Saturday night he headed to Akron, parked the car somewhere, and joined the party. After a few hours it was time to head home—but he'd forgotten where he parked the car. He walked the streets, didn't have any luck, and decided the police would have a better time locating it, so he gave up. Cops eventually came across the car some time later, but not before Milt told the staff that week they were down one news car. Oddly enough, no one asked how he got home.

Dick Kemp had a similar tale. The "Child from Wilde" lived up to his name. He was one of WIXY's most popular and recognizable jocks, and he loved a good party. He got invited to plenty of them, too, with lots of fans pushing each other aside to tip a glass with the "Wilde Childe." He also had a big salary, bonuses, and income from commercials and outside work, but he would only drive junker cars that cost a few bucks. You'd see him show up at events in some rattletrap that left piles of rust as soon as he parked it. Bob Charles used the name Mark Allen when he was with WIXY, and he knew Kemp. One day he asked Kemp why he drove these rolling wrecks, and the Childe told him, "I tend to forget where I park them."

Carl Reese was one of Cleveland's legendary Top 40 jocks. He was your "captain of the morning" at WHK, with one of the smoothest voices in radio. By the late 1980s, Reese landed at WRMR, which was playing the "Music of Your Life" nostalgia format. It was a six-day week for the air staff, and I did news on Carl's Saturday morning show. Three things you could count on: Carl would always bring a huge box of donuts, he would walk around in a skivvy t-shirt, and he'd fill you up with great stories about Cleveland broadcast history, between bites of donuts. That's what made working Saturdays fun for everyone.

One summer weekend I pulled into the station's lot and noticed Carl's trunk was partially open. I mentioned it to him when I went to the studio, and he said he knew. Every fifteen minutes or so, he would walk away from the studio for a few minutes. I did a newscast, then walked in to get a donut. I asked Carl a question, he held up a finger and said "Hold that thought. Come with me." We walked out to the parking lot, he opened the trunk all the way, and inside were two little dogs. They were sitting on blankets and had water and toys, and the started wagging their tails as soon as they saw Carl. He took them out, played with them a little, let them walk around for a minute, and then put them back in the trunk. Then Carl would partially close the trunk. "I couldn't get anyone to watch my dogs so I brought them to work." I asked why he didn't just bring them into the station lobby. It was far enough from the studio that you wouldn't hear them if they started barking. Carl shook his head. "They would do the same thing to the lobby that they did to my living room! They seem to like it in the trunk." From what I saw, they did!

Years later, I was working at WOIO and Carl stopped by for an interview. I mentioned to one of the videographers about the trunk incident, and she later asked Carl if he still went out every fifteen minutes to open his trunk. He asked "How did you know about that?" and said no. He claimed he took an icepick and punched a bunch of holes in the trunk so he didn't have to go out as often. I'm pretty sure he was kidding about that.

Now here are a couple of radio tales that have become legendary within the industry. We don't want to embarrass the individuals involved. They are all top-notch broadcast people, so we won't reveal their names or the stations. Let me just stress that all these stories were told to me by the folks they happened to, and I don't endorse any of the elements that made these stories so unique.

There was a crack news man in town who had a real gift for journalism. He was well informed, could ask insightful questions at the drop of a hat, and was known for breaking stories. Everyone at the other stations respected him for his work in the field. What they didn't respect was his distinct lack of hygiene. He was a single guy with a unique aroma and wavy lines rising from his body. No one wanted to say anything that hurt his feelings, but behind his back he was nicknamed "Stank." At the same station there was a female jock who would get blinding, crippling migraines at a moment's notice. She wouldn't even be able to walk straight, and had to be rushed immediately to the Cleveland Clinic. Vomiting would give her temporary relief, so she could at least function and get to the hospital. In fact, she told me she could vomit at will with no outside stimulation. I asked how she did that and she said, "I imagine I'm in Stank's clothes hamper!" She wasn't joking when she said it either.

Here's that other story.

One of the most recognized news people in town was in demand from other stations and could pretty much write his own ticket. He was also known for high-grade ganja. He wasn't alone. Drugs, and especially marijuana, were evident at just about every station. One older news person had never smoked weed and went to a party where everyone was ten years younger. People were rolling joints and stuffing pipes. "Give me that bowl and I'll fill that hole!" He turned down the flammable stuff but had some brownies that he didn't know had been "seasoned"—and more than a couple. He made it home, didn't know how, and lost his balance and fell on the floor as he was taking off his jacket. His wife called down the steps to see if it was him. He answered "Yes," face-down on the floor, and stayed there until morning. He finished taking his jacket off when he woke up a few hours later.

But about that other news guy, the popular one.

A rival station in town made him a great offer, and he put in his two-week notice. That was late on a Friday, but this guy had to work a Saturday shift. Weekend shifts are a minor nuisance. You had to be there for a few hours, but there was no management or support staff on duty, pretty much just you and the person on the air. That Saturday, he was sitting in a remote news booth that was being redone with foam rubber padding on the walls to soundproof it. He had a brand new bag of weed, his pipe, and a lighter, and he decided it was time for a break. This stuff was supposed to be super-high-powered hooch, too. He packed the pipe and put it in his mouth, and just as he was about to light it he heard a sound in the newsroom. The story has been repeated many times over the years, and some say he hid the stuff behind the foam rubber, some say it was behind a panel in the dropped ceiling, but that's the only variation from telling to telling. It was the station's vice-president who came in specifically to ask, "Is it true you're leaving us?" "Yeah. I put in my two-week notice." Well, in that highly competitive time, such behavior didn't fly. The news guy was told to hand over his key to the station, and he was escorted to the elevator.

Two years later, after a turbulent time at the new place, his contract expired, and he found himself back at the old station working a lazy Saturday shift. He was sitting, bored, in the same news studio, and suddenly it hit him. He went to where he had hidden the weed, and it was still there, including the lighter!

This is not an endorsement of any of that behavior, but it's still funny!

Another incident brought on a wave of uncontrollable laughter, though it was far from funny. In 1977, a jock at WGCL who had family in California went back for a visit. He'd spent some quality time in Haight-Ashbury years before and was very in touch with the West Coast "scene." His brother worked for a major chemical company, and years before had managed to hide 1,000 hits of pure Owsley Stanley LSD in the firm's deep freeze. (When he died in 2011, *The New York Times* called Owsley "The Artisan of Acid." He had mass-produced as many as five million doses of the hallucinogen that was "purer and finer than any other" before or since. Owsley's stuff was not for beginners. Pink Floyd's Syd Barrett sampled Owsley's wares in the late Sixties and never really recovered.) The jock from G98 got a few tabs from his brother as a parting gift and headed back to Cleveland.

The jock passed some on to one of the anchors working upstairs at WERE. He warned him that this was "high octane" LSD and to use it very sparingly. The anchor apparently thought this was a Saturday shift, very little news, no one is really listening and he was on his way home right after the show. This might ease the boredom. Down the hatch. The whole tab!

A short time later, the drug kicked in big time and the anchor started laughing maniacally at every story. It didn't matter. Bank robbery, murder—he couldn't control himself! Word came down to get him off the air now! I recall coming up the steps and seeing him by the coat rack. I wasn't aware what was happening and said "hi" as I got to the top step. The anchor's eyes bugged out of his head, he let out this low, crazy laugh, and I just about fell down the stairs. As he was led away by his ride home I was told what happened. Another day at the office!

There's an old *Saturday Night Live* skit that shows Dan Aykroyd as a jock sitting between two microphones. He would switch back and forth between stations, a high-powered jock on one and a laid-back one on the other. A rule of comedy is that the closer a joke is to reality, the funnier it is, and folks in radio saw this one first hand. In the early Seventies, "Tall Ted" Hallaman was a relaxed jock on WHK, but he would do weekend and overnight news on the sister station WMMS, which at that time was so relaxed it made Hallaman seemed perky. Then there was Lee Andrews. At around that same time he was working as a progressive rock jock on the FM, WNCR, but on his Saturday night shift he would also be on WGAR at the same time. Problem was he had to time records on each station so the breaks were at different times, and that often meant running a good distance between the two studios. Happened again at M105 and WBBG. Dave Sharp was on board one night at the AM, WBBG, when he took a call on the studio hotline. It was Larry "the Diamond Man" Robinson, who owned the station, and he wanted to know why M105 was off the air. Sharp ran to the other studio, and saw the jock passed out from too much booze or drugs or whatever. He ran back to tell the boss, and Sharp says Robinson suggested he "Xerox" himself, because at that point he was running both shows until back-ups came in.

"You're scaring my kids!"

Denny Sanders Got an Earful

MOST PEOPLE THINK OF their radio as a box with a bunch of voices and songs and the occasional commercial or news report. That's obviously not the case. Every station, every show, is a cooperative effort, and the person behind the mic is juggling lots of separate elements to entertain and inform. The best jocks can interact with their audiences and incorporate them in the show, but there's a big variable. Denny Sanders can tell you that "Listeners are sometimes in another world," and he has plenty of scars to prove it.

Sanders came to Cleveland in 1971 from WNTN in Boston. Those were the days when the so-called counterculture was at its peak, and it was pretty easy to get a jock on the phone for a chat between records. Back then WMMS wasn't selling a lot of spots, and the station played some long sets of music so the jocks had plenty of time to talk. The problem is that a lot of folks didn't understand the concept of radio. And there were plenty of whack jobs, too.

"Listeners can be very strange," Sanders recalls from experience. "Once, when Cleveland was being hit with a dangerous tornado touchdown, I went on air with a warning and then repeated it. Someone called the station a few minutes later, demanding that I stop the announcement because 'you're scaring my kids.'"

Then there are the music critics, who, unfortunately, don't always limit their comments to music. Sanders recalls, "Once when I was playing Chuck Berry's 'Johnny B. Goode' on WMMS, some listener calls in and complains about the song, asking me when I was going to play some *real* rock and roll?" Sanders can talk music with anyone, and even in those days of album rock it was

obvious that some important "roots" music was still valid on a progressive rock station. Not this caller. "I told him that Chuck Berry
was about as real as it gets and he replied 'Chuck Berry? What do
n-----s have to do with rock and roll?'" The anonymity of a phone
call went a long way toward drawing out ignorance back then.

That wasn't the only time, either.

Over the years, Sanders saw plenty of change in the audience.

"Toward the end of my time at WMMS, I became quite disillu-
sioned with what happened to some in the album rock audience,"
he says. "What started as an audience that loved the unexpected
and exotic had deteriorated in the 1980s to a conservative crowd
who seemed to dismiss any music that wasn't power-guitar-based,
done in 4/4 time and played in a major key by a bunch of white
males. We were lucky at WMMS because we always mixed in some
R&B, reggae and oldies and we held our ground pretty well, but we
still took a lot of crap from certain factions of the audience, some of
it tinged with the ugly brush of racism. Once, after playing (I think)
Hendrix into the Isley Brothers into Bob Marley, I got a call from
some guy who asked me if I realized that I just played three black
people in a row. I told him that I hadn't noticed, and he laughed
and said 'Well you should notice. After all, WMMS is supposed to
be a white station, right? Don't let it happen again,' and he hung
up. Sickening!"

Face-to-face encounters were a whole different animal.

"Being a public person sometimes ain't what it's cracked up to
be," Sanders recalls. "I was on air in Cleveland for thirty years, and
especially during the WMMS days in the 1970s and 1980s, my
name was pretty well known around Cleveland at that time. But
I will tell you that fame, even the miniature fame of local radio,
is a double-edged sword. Most of the time, people were very nice
and just wanted to say hello or ask a question. However, once in
a while, you would run into someone at a party—who was usually
drunk—who felt like screwing with you. At one such event, some
guy walked, or should I say, staggered, up to me and said, out of the
blue 'Denny Sanders, huh? I bet you think your shit doesn't stink.'

You meet some real characters when you work in radio, and Denny Sanders met more than his share in his thirty-plus years on the air. *Janet Macoska*

Trying to lighten him up, I assured him that it certainly did, but he wouldn't let up. He began hurling more insults at me, so I simply walked away. 'Big man! Big Man! There goes the big man! Too stuck up to talk to a mere mortal like me,' he yelled. 'You egotistical bastard!' The guy was going absolutely hysterical!"

And then, a godsend for anonymous critics—the Internet! Sanders took his lumps there, too.

"As I was wrapping up my radio career in 2001, those silly local radio chat boards on the net were just starting up. I never paid much attention to them, but one day a friend cut-pasted a couple of threads about me and sent them along. I had just been let go as Head of Programming and Operations at WMJI after thirteen years, primarily because my new corporate boss and I just didn't see eye to eye about the direction of the station, even though it was setting records in ratings and revenue. Besides, I never fit in with the sophomoric frat-boy culture of Clear Channel at the time, who recently bought the station.

"Anyway," Sanders continues, "the posts on the radio chat board from people who supposedly knew the inside story of my departure were so completely ridiculous! I mean way, *way* out there. And others would chime in saying 'yes, that's what I heard, too.' Over the course of several days, I kept reading that I was 'making the rounds of every station in town, begging and pleading for a job.' People would list sightings of me in station lobbies that I had never set foot in. Hilarious. What motivates people to write such claptrap is beyond me. Sometimes I wonder how real stars like film actors or TV personalities keep their sanity when they go shopping with their kids and see some ugly, made-up story about them on the front page of one of those supermarket tabloids complete with a phony, Photoshopped picture.

"That part of my former life, I don't miss a single bit."

"Bouncy, Bouncy!"

Jimi Hendrix Meets an Alien in Cleveland

CHUCK DUNAWAY HAD A career to talk about well before he came to Cleveland. He worked at top stations in Dallas, Houston, and New York, but hit the mother lode when he landed on the shores of Lake Erie. You may remember Dunaway from WIXY 1260, but his first gig in town was up the dial at WKYC, and what a run he had.

1100 was a 50,000-watt powerhouse that could be heard over most of the continental U.S. and Canada. AM radio was still king of the hill, and most of the big rock shows that came through town were all sponsored by WKYC and WIXY. The jocks had a finger on the pulse of their audience. As the British Invasion faded away, there was a new, spacier music coming out of England and the West Coast. The big record labels took notice, signed up a bunch of the most popular bands and put them on a road that eventually brought them to Cleveland. We're not talking about the bands that were really out there, like Ultimate Spinach or Lothar and the Hand People—acts that would find homes on college radio or the upcoming progressive FM formats. These were acts that could produce hits and still maintain their credibility. Dunaway has vivid memories of three in particular.

He'd heard from friends up north about this guy who was doing some really weird things with a guitar. "I heard that Jimi Hendrix was huge in Detroit. I called the Belkin brothers, who were friends of mine, and told them to investigate bringing him to Cleveland. They did, and the perk for WKYC was that we could put the call letters on the show. We sold tickets, the Belkins did, in the lobby of our radio station." Those were the days before services like Ticket-

Cleveland police had their hands full trying to keep fans out of the
WKYC building when Jimi Hendrix stopped by for a visit. *George Shuba*

ron. You could go into a Burrows bookstore, they'd look under the
cash drawer in the register, and you could take your pick.

When the Hendrix shows were announced for March 1968,
there were plenty of people stopping by WKYC for tickets and, as
Dunaway recalls, "Since I was the guy who brought it all together
for the Belkins, they arranged an interview for me!"

The day of the show Jimi Hendrix and his bass player walked
into the WKYC studio.

"Jimi was very mild-mannered, very quiet," according to

Dunaway. "Very polite, too. Noel Redding came with him, and he was very quiet. He just sat there and Jimi did all the talking. Hendrix introduced tunes and we gave away some albums." Meanwhile, there was a growing crowd trying to get in the door, and the cops had their hands full. Hendrix, Redding, and Dunaway looked down with a smile.

"There were quite a few people outside the radio station. We were on the second floor, and people on the ground level were looking up. We started throwing stuff out the window to them. The station had a 'love beads' promotion at that time that was a big deal. Hundreds of them, and we were throwing them at the crowd." They got a disgusted look from the cops, as if to sneer, "Thanks a lot for the help!"

It wasn't long before the police herded the crowds away from the station. It was almost show time, and the opening act, Soft Machine, was due any minute. The streets were cleared, and it seemed silly to take a limo five hundred feet down East Sixth Street. "After the interview," Dunway says, "we walked from the radio studio to Music Hall's backstage entrance down the street. Maybe a block away." It was that casual.

"[Hendrix] was a quiet guy off-stage, but when he put on that guitar, he was on fire. I emceed the show that night and wow! Even though he was playing Music Hall he was pretty big by the time we brought him in. Getting bigger, too. Two shows, and one of them was stopped by a bomb scare. When Jimi came out for the first show some kid yelled, 'Take off your hat!' and Jimi shot back, 'Take off your pants!' His pick hit the strings, and the place exploded!"

Dunaway recalls there was a lot of tension on the streets in those days. "Hippies, police, racial stuff, but that stopped at the door of the Music Hall that night. Keep in mind that Hendrix was a black guy playing in Cleveland to an all-white audience. Plus, nobody had ever seen an act like that. He hunched over and put his guitar between his legs. Humping his amps. Really wild!"

You may be interested in a couple of stories that happened before and during the show. The band had flown into Cleveland the night before, and Dunaway went with a friend to keep Hendrix occupied. "We pretty much just hung out. Went out to eat, that sort of thing. Talked a lot in the off hours . . . and he bought a Corvette in Cleveland! He met a girl at Otto's Grotto at the Statler the night before his show. He came in a day early and we went to the club and I introduced him to this girl. Turned out she was a car salesperson for a downtown Chevrolet dealer. Hendrix took her up to his room and, uh, got to know her. Meanwhile, the writer Joe Eszterhas and me were sitting in the living room of his two-room suite. They finished their business and the next day he went out and bought a car from her."

Then there was a visit with an "alien."

"Leonard Nimoy was in town promoting *Star Trek,* and he stopped by WKYC for an interview. I happened to mention that Hendrix was coming in that week, and Nimoy said, 'Really? I've heard a lot about him! Love to meet him.' I told him to stay in town an extra day and we'll get you backstage. He showed up, we got the two together, and they both enjoyed saying hello."

Nimoy watched the shows from the side of the stage and Dunaway even brought him out to say hello to the crowd. Mr. Spock and Jimi Hendrix at the same concert! Years later Nimoy recalled that meeting and said Hendrix was a sci-fi freak who loved the show. He suggested Hendrix could do a walk-on as alien in one of the episodes and he loved the idea! Numbers were exchanged but they couldn't sync up their schedules. It would have been the most famous science fiction TV show ever!

People tend to get a little out of control at concerts, on both sides of the stage. These shows were no different, and Dunaway recalls, "Somebody was drunk backstage, not Hendrix or Nimoy, and we were all walking down this metal staircase and the guy goes flying forward. We stood there for a second and one of them, Hendrix or Nimoy, just said, 'Bouncy bouncy!'"

There was a crowd on the streets, too, and they decided to make a run for the station. "After the show we walked back to WKYC, and one guy grabbed my hairpiece! He took a good piece of my hair with it. This guy thought he scalped me!" They promised to get together again when Hendrix was back in Cleveland. Sadly, he would never return.

Then there's the case of Jim Morrison and the Doors.

"Yeah, I met and spent time with them. Most of them, anyway. Jim Morrison was a talent, but he was also a major drunk. We had a show scheduled at Public Hall and no one could find Morrison. He's an hour and a half late, and the crowd is getting rowdy. We went out to find him, and it turns out he was sitting in a bar getting drunk. He was sitting there knocking back drinks with a Merchant Marine he just met. After a while, there's a knock on the backstage door and it's Morrison and this sailor. They walked in, and Morrison slurred, 'This is the stage manager. Whatever he says goes. Just do it!' Morrison walked on stage, he could barely stand up, and mayhem reigned."

Another time, Dunaway recalls, "Janis Joplin was here on a bill with Big Brother & the Holding Company and Country Joe and the Fish. She and I got tight because we were both from Texas, but it went beyond that. I worked in Houston, and I told her there was a lady from Beaumont who called my show every night asking to hear her songs on KILT. I asked why she was such a Janis fan, and she said, 'I'm her Mom!' She looked at me and you could tell in her eyes that it really touched her. We spent the night talking about Houston"—over a bottle of Southern Comfort. Joplin also enjoyed exploring the dark recesses of Public Hall and brought Dunaway along as a tour guide.

Jimi Hendrix died in September 1970, and a few weeks later, Janis Joplin was gone. By July the next year, Jim Morrison met the same tragic end. They all were 27 when they died. Fortunately, their memories live on.

Dunaway wasn't long for 1100, either. WIXY 1260 had one-tenth the power of WKYC, 5000 watts, but ratings-wise, they dominated the market. WKYC couldn't match WIXY's promotional muscle. Station managers would drive to Cleveland, listen or tape as much as they could of WIXY programming, and try to copy as many ideas as possible.

In early 1969, NBC pulled the plug on WKYC's Top 40 format.

But the top dogs at WIXY knew talent, and they hired Chuck Dunaway to "cross the street" and take over as both afternoon drive jock and program director. This was a golden age for WIXY, drawing tens of thousands of people for Hot Pants contests, Christmas parades, and even the Cleveland debut of the controversial Broadway hit *Hair*. Dunaway discovered that he liked the management role, and after a successful run at WIXY he headed out to run and own stations across the south. These days he's back in Texas, but chances are that every now and then Dunaway can close his eyes and remember some remarkable times in Cleveland radio.

The Birth of the Buzzard

WE END THIS VOLUME with a look at the birth of a Cleveland radio icon, as told by its creator, David Helton . . .

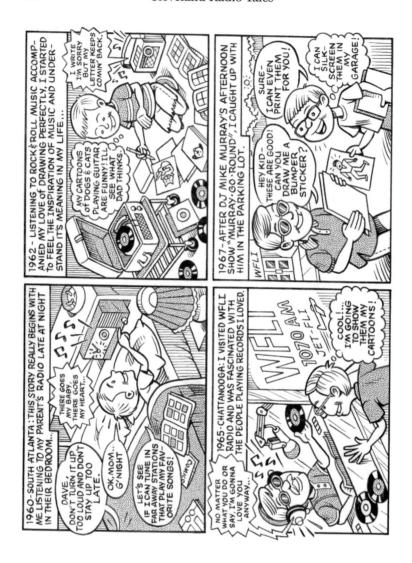

TO BE CONT.-

Acknowledgments

A SPECIAL NOD TO Daniel Alvarez, Opie Anderson, Trixie Andrus, Teddy Bellar, Shanie Burwell, Augie Kopkas, Willie Little, Marley Mona, Daisy Misciagna, Happy & Heidi Olszewski, Tico Pruchinski, Timmy Springborn, and Louie Wheeler.

We also want to offer special thanks to Cliff Baechle, Frank Foti, Brad Funk, Eric Funk, Rick Funk, David Gray, Pam Hanson, David Helton, Bianca Kontra, Tom Kontra, Jane Lassar, Angelina Leas, Milton Maltz, Jenny Misciagna, Cate Misciagna, Cole Misciagna, Cora Misciagna, Theresa Misciagna, Tony Misciagna, Denny Sanders, and John Webster.

OTHER BOOKS OF INTEREST . . .

OTHER BOOKS OF INTEREST . . .

Cleveland Rock and Roll Memories
True and Tall Tales of the Glory Days, Told by Musicians, DJs, Promoters, and Fans Who Made the Scene in the '60s, '70s, and '80s

Carlo Wolff

Clevelanders who grew up with Rock and Roll in the 1960s, '70s, and '80s remember a golden age, with clubs like the Agora, trendsetting radio stations WIXY 1260 and WMMS, Coffee Break Concerts, The World Series of Rock. Includes first-person stories by fans, musicians, DJs, reporters, club owners, and more, with rare photos and memorabilia.

Ghoulardi
Inside Cleveland TV's Wildest Ride

Tom Feran, R. D. Heldenfels

The behind-the-scenes story of the outrageous Ghoulardi show and its unusual creator, Ernie Anderson. The groundbreaking late-night TV horror host shocked and delighted Northeast Ohio in the mid-1960s on Friday nights with strange beatnik humor, bad movies, and innovative sight gags. Includes rare photos, interviews, transcripts, and trivia.

"Captures a hint of the mania that made Ghoulardi a Cleveland idol in a sleepy era before long hair, drugs, assassinations, war and protests." – Columbus Dispatch

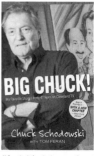

Big Chuck!
My Favorite Stories from 47 Years on Cleveland TV

Chuck Schodowski, Tom Feran

A beloved Cleveland TV legend tells funny and surprising stories from a lifetime in television. "Big Chuck" collaborated with Ernie Anderson on the groundbreaking "Ghoulardi" show and continued to host a late-night show across four decades—the longest such run in TV history. Packed with behind-the-scenes details about TV and celebrities.

"A vivid picture of an honest man in the insane world of television. Highly recommended." – Midwest Book Review

Read samples at **www.grayco.com**